ALL WELL

HOW TO SEW CLOTHES

Learn with intuitive,
super-hackable patterns

BOX TOP
front & back body
cut 1 each on fold

fold / gr

Amelia Greenhall and Amy Bornman
Photography by Christine Armbruster and Tara Bennett

ALL WELL

HOW TO SEW CLOTHES

Learn with intuitive, super-hackable patterns

ABRAMS, NEW YORK

All Well is a collaboration between Amy Bornman and Amelia Greenhall, based in Pittsburgh and Seattle. We would like to acknowledge that Pittsburgh occupies ancestral lands of the Osage Nation and Shawnee Tribe and that Seattle is the traditional land of the first people of Seattle, the Duwamish People past and present, and we honor with gratitude the land itself and the Osage, Shawnee, and Duwamish Tribes.

PHOTOS: Christine Armbruster, christinearmbruster.com; Tara Bennett, tarabennettphotography.com; Amy Bornman; Amelia Greenhall

THANK YOU: Sarah Stephens, Adam Greenhall, C. Scott, Isaiah Bornman, our families, friends, and everyone who has sewn All Well patterns.

hello@allwellworkshop.com
allwellworkshop.com
ameliagreenhall.com
amybornman.com

Editor: Shawna Mullen
Design Manager: Jenice Kim
Managing Editor: Glenn Ramirez
Production Manager: Kathleen Gaffney

Designed by Sebit Min

Library of Congress Control Number: 2022933913

ISBN: 978-1-4197-6202-4
eISBN: 978-1-64700-677-8

Cover © 2023 Abrams

Printed and bound in China
10 9 8 7 6 5 4

Abrams books are available at special discounts when purchased in quantity for premiums and promotions as well as fundraising or educational use. Special editions can also be created to specification. For details, contact specialsales@abramsbooks.com or the address below.

Abrams® is a registered trademark of Harry N. Abrams, Inc.

ABRAMS The Art of Books
195 Broadway, New York, NY 10007
abramsbooks.com

Contents

Sewing and Abundance

This book is about sewing clothes and bags—which is probably why you picked it up. But we wanted to tell you right from the start that this book is also about something else, a thing that is bigger and ultimately more important (dare we say) than sewing. It is about *abundance* first, and *sewing* second, though it might seem the other way around as you work your way through. This book is about using sewing as a way to practice and gather up abundance, to wear it on your body out into the day. It's a book about doing something like sewing because it *means* something to you—and about *how* to do it gently and with enthusiasm. It's about learning something new without too much expectation of how it will turn out, beyond sinking into a process and seeing what happens. It's about clothes and wearing them, and about fingers and eyes and minds and souls. It's about your life in its glittery particularity, the ways it's only yours—and about ours, Amelia's and Amy's: the lives we're writing from, our own details and interiors. It's about community, and the things you do when you're all alone in your home, quietly huddled over a sewing machine. This is a book about abundance—*and* sewing!

We all wear clothes every day, all have to solve the problem of *what do I want to wear?* We'd like to offer the opinion that when you sew your own clothes you can end up with ones that feel better to wear than ones you can buy. Abundance in sewing looks like welcoming the practice of sewing into your life, gently, thoughtfully, and allowing it to mean something to you. It looks like making clothes that are personal, well-fitted, versatile. It looks like using materials that are hard-wearing, sustainable, easy to wash and mend. It looks like filling wardrobe holes and finding garments that work together in lots of ways. It looks like learning to use simple shapes and basic sewing techniques improvisationally (with some guidance) for endless riffing. Using the patterns and instructions included in this book, you can sew yourself a box top, a dress, a cardigan coat or jacket—and many nearly endless variations and hacks built on those foundational simple shapes, to mix and match into a full wardrobe of outfits. Plus a whole slew of bags to wear and use with all the clothes you make.

If you can sew a straight line, you can sew anything. (And we'll teach you how to sew a straight line!) We will help you get started from scratch, if that's what you're doing. We'll teach you how to set up a workshop even if you have no space and a small budget, give advice if you need to figure out what machine and tools to buy, and talk about how to get oriented once you have what you need. We'll give you lots of detailed instructions and illustrations for certain sewing skills and techniques that, with a little practice, will become second nature for you later on. We will explain *why* you're doing things, and when it is important to do things a certain way, or take more care, and when you can improvise or not worry too much about precision.

We'll tell you what you need to know to sew some clothes—nothing new, nothing revolutionary, just a way through the inevitable and sometimes intimidating decision-making process that comes with sewing. How to choose fabrics, how to read the markings on the pattern to properly cut out and mark pattern pieces, how to sew them together, how to use your iron to press in the special sewing way, how to backstitch and zigzag. How to assess fit, learn from what you make, how to learn more from other sources and follow what feels exciting. And, of course, we'll share the small tips we have in our own toolboxes, what we've learned along the way—trying to gather up the things we wish we knew when we were learning to sew, the book we wish we'd had when we were starting.

This book is about how to cultivate sewing as a *practice*—how to start, how to continue, how to weave it into your days. How to pay attention to what you want to wear, how to find the fabrics you love and the shapes you're drawn to, how to choose what to sew next and how to use your scraps, how to be economical. Once you learn to sew, it's something that is always with you to pick up or put down, learning and growing along the way, letting it unravel at your own pace. Sewing is centering, giving you small goals to achieve slowly and in your own time, a place to solve problems with low stakes, a way to practice mending, both literally and figuratively. Like what we eat, what we read,

what we do, what we see—what we choose to wear and where that garment comes from *matters*, implicates more than just our outward appearance. Sewing is a skill *and* an art form. Abundance in sewing lies at the intersection of the two: the simple physical act of making stitches in fabric combining with the things you bring to it that are unique to you—your own hands, your own mind, your own body, your own life—to make clothes that are more than *just* clothes, something to wear, but ones that are truly one of a kind.

Sewing is deeply practical but it can also be poetic, if we let it. An invitation to find new appreciation for the beauty and detail in fabric and construction and the way things go together and are connected to everything else.

As your sewing practice grows, you might find yourself feeling even more at home in your body and with the things you use daily that you've made or that someone else made that found their way to you—like clothes, bags, and other small soft things. For us, we've found that the confidence from the skilled work of sewing and wearing comfortable clothes spills over into the rest of life, helping to bring clarity about what we want and how we want to show up and contribute to the world and to our own circumstances. It's about abundance, with sewing as the way in. Hopefully you find some of that in this book. We're really glad you're here.

box top

box top

long sleeve box top

ruffle

box dress

long sleeve ruffle dress

cardigan coat

cardigan

cardigan jacket

cardigan jacket

cardigan coat

quil

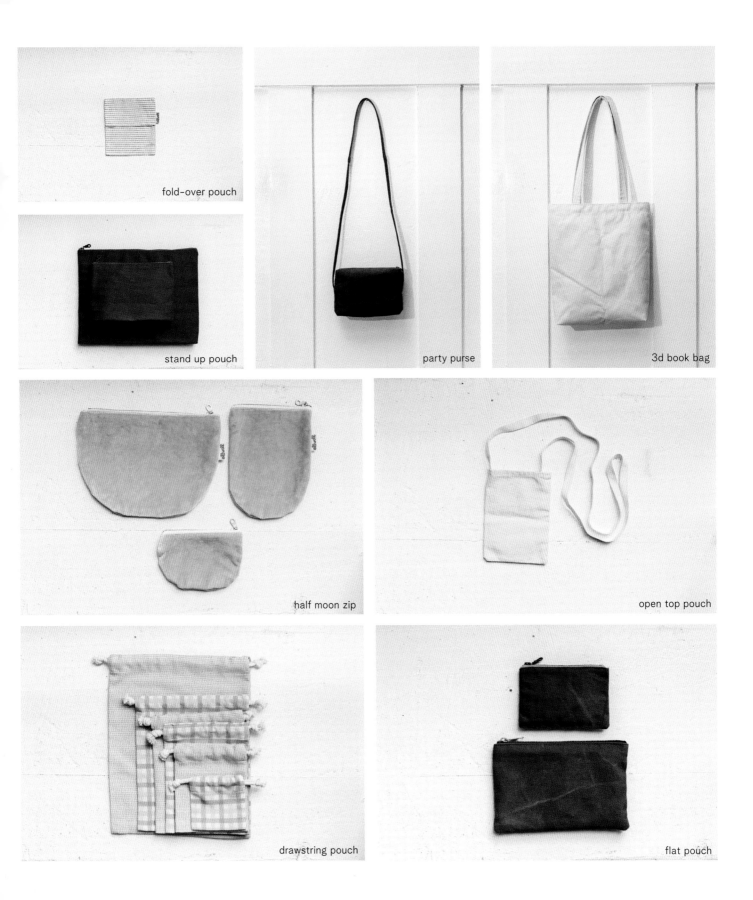

fold-over pouch

stand up pouch

party purse

3d book bag

half moon zip

open top pouch

drawstring pouch

flat pouch

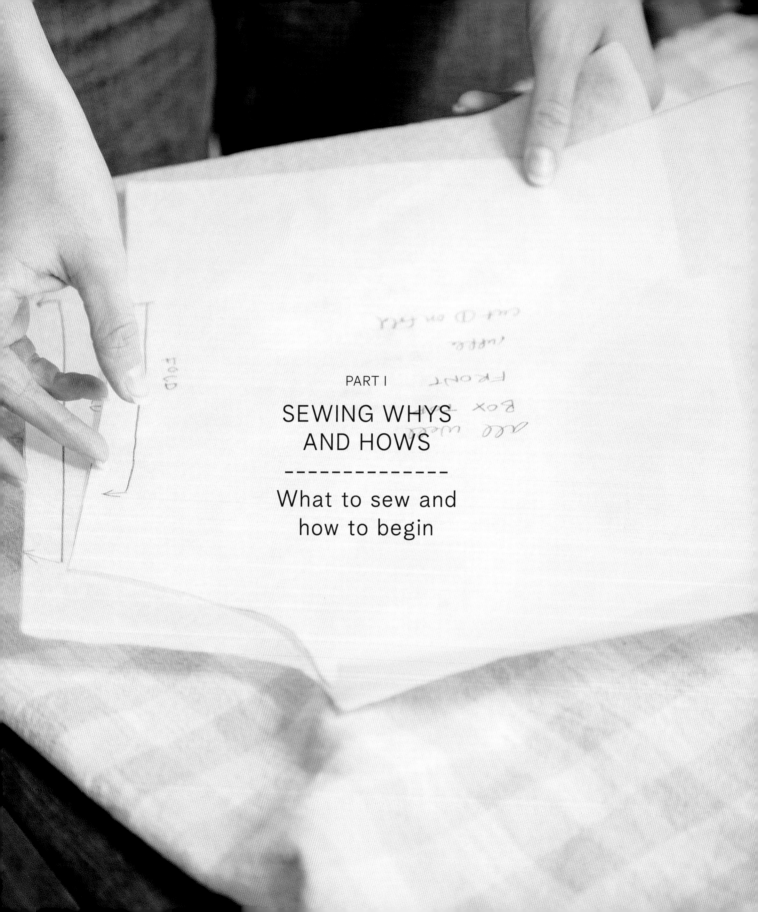

PART I

SEWING WHYS AND HOWS

What to sew and
how to begin

Chapter 1

What You Might Want to Sew, and How, and Why

simple clothes

AMY: The first garment you sew tends to be unforgettable, even if not fully successful—mine was a tank top with a gathered neckline, sewn from soft gray cotton with black threads woven into a grid that I picked out at JOANN. I can remember almost everything about making it, which is unusual for me. I had been dabbling in figuring out patchwork quilting for a few weeks, setting up and putting to use the sewing machine I'd received as a wedding present, but the idea of making *clothes* enthralled and intimidated me at once. I took my time before beginning— lurking on Instagram, mulling over patterns, folding and unfolding my few yards of fabric. One day, I just went for it. I made a top. I put it on. I walked out of my apartment in the top I'd made. I was *wearing* it.

It felt incredible. I liked what I had made. I'd done it deliberately, thoughtfully, and I *liked* it! I felt good wearing it. I wanted to make more clothes, nearly immediately feeling the creative itch. It was really as simple as that. I made it, I wore it, I liked it, I wanted to make and wear more. I wasn't immediately good, and I hadn't made something perfect. I just liked it. Believe me when I say that it was very, *very* imperfect. I used white thread that didn't blend in well with the gray fabric. I had somewhat messed up the gathers. I didn't know yet that I should do anything to

finish the raw edges of the interior seams. If you were to look closely at this top (which I still frequently wear), you would see that it is somewhat shoddily sewn and very ordinary looking—but it was mine. I made it! Some door in me unlocked, and I walked through to somewhere new.

I've always liked wearing simple clothes best, which is nice because I like *sewing* simple clothes best too. I like to not have to think too hard when I sew. Though my work is to teach others about sewing, I don't know *everything* about it. When something complicated's going on, I'm googling. But I've always felt most grounded in simplicity in every corner of my life, giving the best of myself to what is ordinary.

All Well, the sewing pattern design studio Amelia and I collaborate to run, was built in this same spirit. We both love to design and teach simple clothes. It follows that all of the patterns in this book could be characterized as "simple." You might not be into simple—that's fine! The amazing thing about simple is that it can very quickly become complex, even secretly, even in little ways. Really, that's the project of this book—to start simple, the trunk of a tree, and see all the possibilities growing up and away like branches, and leaves, and buds.

AMELIA: Sewing things made of simple shapes in endless combinations fills some deep artist-need for me. I like to sew for the same reason I like to cook: It's satisfying to make things. Here are the techniques and skills, here are the tools and materials: so many ways they can go together to fit a mood or need or desire. Cookbooks taught me how to cook meals, and also how to manage an inventory over time, work with a budget, source resourcefully and share, and not to waste. Adam and I mostly cook simple meals at home, variations on the same basic concepts, choosing by season and what's around. I remember reading cooking blogs and being surprised by the recipes that were just an encouragement to eat bread and chocolate together, or radishes and butter and salt. Sometimes it's really that plain with cooking, and sewing can be like that too. I'm thinking about the box top, or the simple pouches in this book: One or two square-ish pieces of cloth go together and are transformed, fairly quickly, into something useful and also nice.

My first attempts at learning to sew my own clothes were mostly frustrating, not anything I wanted to wear. I kept returning to it, feeling a pull. Over time my skills grew: learning to adjust patterns, building up technical skill in my hands, having patience for reading the instructions, and developing an intuition of how garments were made. I spent money and time, slowly building up more specialized tools and skills. I figured out how important picking fabrics is, for bags as well as clothes. I began to love making complicated and slow things also. Like learning to make croissants and lemon tarts, pickling lemons and shallots, or rolling out ravioli. Yes to box tops, also yes to fitted pants with darts and pockets and belt loops and a zipper fly and buttonholes. But it's always the simple things that I sew and wear the most, and that's what we're talking about in this book. Simple clothes can take you far.

about the patterns in this book

When you first look at the patterns in this book, you will notice that they are decidedly uncomplicated. Simple shapes, not very many pieces to cut, a pared-down sewing method, as straightforward as possible. There are forks in the road and places where you get to make choices about your own body and your own life, how you think the garment you're making will fit in your own wardrobe, or how you can customize a bag to suit what you want to use it for. You will build skills and instincts to help you sew confidently and improvisationally with every pattern you approach.

Just because the patterns are simple doesn't mean they can't become nuanced and complex garments, and part of a cohesive wardrobe. That's what's so beautiful about simple clothes, really—the way they can fit together into something really personal and interesting. Beyond sewing, so much thought and creativity goes into the fabrics you choose, the way they fit on your body, the way you style together the things you make. Simple

clothes don't mean you have a simple wardrobe—and that's a wonderful thing.

hacking and improvisation

This book is different from a lot of sewing books and patterns in another important way: It's designed for hacking. You can learn a lot by following all the rules a sewing pattern gives you—you can also learn a lot by breaking those rules. That's what gave us the idea of making hacking guides to accompany our garment patterns—what if hacking (deviating from the written pattern, in small or big ways) was the norm, an encouragement from one maker to another to find *your* garment within the template of the pattern?

We'll try to give you guidance about where you're free to riff and where it's best to stay on the trail. We'll give you ideas, instructions, and lots of options: Follow your gut and choose what feels good to you. For every pattern in this book, you have our explicit permission to do literally whatever you want with it. Make choices—even ones you think we might not agree with! We're serious! Follow your ideas wherever they take you!

AMY: The first few times I hacked a sewing pattern, I felt a little nervous about it, like I was going against the designer's intent. But also daring and curious, at least enough to follow through with my off-the-beaten-path ideas. As soon as I tried on my hacked garment and saw the way the choices I made suited *my* body, *my* wardrobe, *my* personal style, I felt energized and really excited. Sewing felt creative to begin with, but now I'd made something that was completely my own! This feeling felt so enlivening that I learned to draft my own patterns, and All Well was born.

tops

Tops were the first garments we made, and it's always where we recommend people start for sewing clothes. A top is a somewhat low-stakes project, especially when you're using a simple pattern that isn't too fitted. It's not a ton of fabric, lots of fabrics will work well, and you can start and finish in a single afternoon if you want to. You can put on your favorite pair of pants and then try on your top to see how it worked out—a magical moment! This is why we love it when we hear that our box top pattern was someone's first ever garment sewing project. Even better, when we hear that they went on to make more versions after their first, catching a whiff of new ideas on the edge of the wind, a hunger that builds as they make something that works. That's *exactly* what we designed it to be: A simple top that can be worn on its own or as a versatile layer, a diving board from which each person who sews it can swan dive into creative sewing, whether for the first or hundredth time.

jackets

We love wearing layers, so we love sewing layers. It's one thing to make *one* garment you love—it's quite another to make *two* and wear them in combination. You might think of jackets as complicated (and they *can* be), but we love to keep them in the "simple" category in our minds—thinking of them as a way to layer, add texture, and add warmth to an outfit. In some ways, jackets can become even more of a uniform than tops—you may own fewer of them but wear each jacket more often than other individual garments in your repertoire. You might have a cardigan you hang on the back of your chair and pop over everything—that's the idea! Coats, cardigans, or "cardigan coats" are not much more complicated to sew than a top, and they are wardrobe all-stars that get a ton of wear (and give extra satisfaction for having made something so useful and cozy).

pants

You won't find any pants patterns in this book (So much to say! So little room!) but we still want to put in a pitch for sewing a pair of your own pants if you like to wear them. It's incredible how GOOD it feels to have pants that fit—you might realize, like Amelia did, that you've never quite had pants that truly fit before. There's a difference between pants you can fit *into* and ones that really fit the particularity of your body, and that feeling is quite worth the learning curve of sorting out fitting adjustments. You may want to start with elastic-waist pants with a roomy, flowy fit, and give yourself some practice making pants themselves before you venture (if ever) into form-fitting jeans or slacks or trousers. Who doesn't want a flowy linen or raw silk or silk pair of lounge pants? In any case, this is just an encouragement to not delay too long on pants, even if they've been seeming intimidating to you.

dresses

The joy of dresses! So much room for beautiful fabrics and prints. So many possibilities and moods: Are you lounging, are you biking around town, are you going to eat with friends, are you at a party? Is it your birthday? A good thing about simple dresses like boxy or ruffly ones is that they don't take much fitting, and flow with your body, and can be nice and cool when it's hot out. A dress in black linen can take you almost anywhere. This book has several dress options, all of them simple, all of them hacks that build on the other skills you will learn. The box dress is a simple tunic, just extending the line of the top down to whatever length you want: Above the knee, at the knee, or even longer. You can add side slits to give yourself room to stride. The ruffle dress is a variation on the ruffle top, just lengthening the ruffle. So fun and twirly! And of course, you can add pockets, or a belt, or sleeves—lots of options that riff on the same foundations but make outfits that feel really different to wear.

complicated and specialized clothes

For all our talk of simple clothes, you might be like—"Okay, Amy and Amelia, but I want to make a button-down shirt with a collar and a pleat." That's an exciting and amazing goal! Complicated clothes are really incredible. Have you ever looked closely at the inside of a suit under the lining? Or at the detail of classic Levi's five-pocket jeans? Or at the beading or darts or seams on a gown? Complicated clothes are very possible to make yourself. They just often require a few things: lots of time, a few specialized tools and materials, and several new skills.

If you're interested in complicated clothes, you will find lots of people to teach you and get into it with you out there in the wide world of sewing. Maybe you want to try to sew some underwear (not hard, but requires different kinds of fabric and different skills than sewing with woven fabric), or specialized clothes for a sport or hobby you love (will often require a particular fabric or design elements to make them suit their function). Those are awesome things to learn to sew, but you won't find that info in this book. Just want to let you know that now.

bags

We love sewing bags. It's so satisfying; they're so useful, and a little more of a sure thing because you don't have to worry about whether they will fit your body or not. Often you're using a sturdier fabric with an easy-to-see grain, like a canvas, which is easy to work with and practice new techniques on. And often bags use less fabric than a garment, making them a little less expensive, easier to handle, and faster to sew. If you've never sewn *at all* before, after testing out some stitches on scrap fabric you might want to sew some of the bags before the clothes. The simple pouches are great because you can make a size for just about anything, the book bags are handy for toting things around, and you can never have too many zip pouches! Bag patterns are a perfect way to practice reading a pattern, cutting out material, sewing, finishing, and pressing.

A bag can truly be a daily companion in a way that a garment can't quite be. Our favorite bags go with us *everywhere*, and they need to feel just right. It's amazing to get to make bags that are custom-fitted to what they will hold, what you need them for, and what kinds of days they'll be up against, and it's really fun to draft new sizes and make them just as you like.

what do you really like to wear?

Think about your favorite clothes—the ones you wear first when they're fresh from laundry day. Your tried-and-trues, the ones you pack for every trip. That top, those pants, that perfect sweater. Or maybe you haven't found or collected all your favorites yet, they're out of reach for one reason or another, but you can imagine them.

If you group together all your favorite clothes, do you see a color palette emerging? A type of fabric? A shape? A certain way things fit? A kind of garment? A theme, a print, a correlation? Those are the sorts of clothes you can aim to make. Clothes inspired by those clothes, clothes that coordinate, contrast, can layer with, and go over or under those clothes.

With everything you sew, do it with those favorite clothes in mind. Let your favorite clothes help you buy fabric, choose patterns, build your projects from the bottom up.

Look at those clothes when you're looking for inspiration when it comes to *ease* and *fabric*—two critical elements of sewing clothes (more about them in Chapter 5.)

gardening and birthday cake

You can get clothes from so many places, made so many ways—any kind of clothing you can conceive of, you can find somewhere. It's so easy to buy clothes that the question, "Why would I sew?" is a deeply honest and logical one that's worth asking even if the answer feels simple. Sewing takes more time, it's not necessarily cheaper, more could go wrong—terribly inefficient compared to buying clothes. It's easy to *not* sew, but you've picked up this book because something about sewing feels interesting to you.

You can think of sewing like gardening or baking a birthday cake. You can buy your vegetables from the market or your cake from the bakery, or you can learn how to grow or make them. It's optional (usually), but meaningful (usually). You don't have to sew your own clothes, but you can. It will take time, and money. It will be messy. It's sometimes inefficient. But there's something satisfying about it—like there's something satisfying about gardening, about baking—even when clothes, vegetables, and cakes are pretty easy to come by. *Even* when the bugs get the tomatoes or the cake is crumbly. How it feels, how it makes you feel, matters. If you asked a baker why they bake, I expect they'd tell you something about how baking makes them feel. Sewing is no different. It doesn't have to feel that way every time you do it, but holistically there's a feeling. If you love something, someone, you know what I mean.

so why do *you* sew your own clothes, Amy and Amelia?

AMY: I was flailing around after I graduated from college with a theater degree. I was young and newly married, living in Chicago, working as a nanny, writing a blog no one read, and interning in theaters for short, unsatisfying spurts—all of which in combination left me feeling bewildered and very small. I couldn't figure out what to do with myself until I started to sew, sort of on a whim. I was inspired by the handmade quilt my husband's grandmother gave us as a wedding gift. One day I thought, *I think I could make that.* So I set out to try. I learned embroidery first (saw some cool stuff on Pinterest I wanted to figure out), then patchwork, and finally I learned to sew clothes (which felt daunting). Sewing was something to do, something to give myself over to in a time when it seemed like there wasn't really a place for me and my work in the world. It gave me new energy, a gentle push forward. Soon, I was sewing nightly, and talking everyone's ear off about sewing. I would go to my barista job at 6 a.m. and doodle pattern ideas on receipt paper. I started making my own sewing patterns, sewing stuff out of old bedsheets, playing with shapes. I started to love getting dressed. I gathered skills and experience until all the personal work started to feel like it was adding up to something. After a little while, friends came to me wanting to learn. I realized other people were curious about what I was up to. For the first time in all my vocational seeking, it felt like a door was swinging wide open to me rather than shutting and locking tight. Sewing became more than a personal hobby—it became a way to be of service and in conversation with other people, which is all I really wanted out of work and life.

Sewing has shifted for me over time—especially as it moved from being a deeply personal hobby to being a job, something I talk about publicly and have a responsibility toward. I am constantly reevaluating my feelings about it—sometimes it feels exciting, sometimes it feels overwhelming or alienating, sometimes I want to do *anything* else. But when it comes time to really actually sit down and sew something for myself or for my family, I feel that old feeling come back—a return to center, a gentle push forward. It feels like magic, and like satisfaction, to spend a few hours sewing and then walk away wearing what I've made. I think I needed to feel powerful in that way in the time in my life when I started sewing, and right now too. To have a space to play, to take risks and control, to accomplish small discrete tasks that add up to something tangible and beautiful.

AMELIA: I love the feeling of wearing clothes that are just as I imagined: warm and dark and sturdy, soft, layered, or translucent. I had ideas that I knew I couldn't find in a store, and sewing my own clothes was part of the artist's life I imagined: climbing mountains and cooking and biking and having adventures with friends, reading lots of books, making art, and publishing and collaborating. I'd be growing kitchen herbs and making sourdough bread and wearing clothes I'd sewn myself. I wanted to feel like myself, I wanted to be comfortable, I wanted to do something about the climate crisis.

I grew up sewing little pencil pouches and pillowcases and doll clothes with a little sewing kit I carried around. I watched my mom and Grandma Jo sew almost anything, and I liked making simple things to solve a problem at hand: A pouch or sleeve in just the right size, an ultralight backpacking sleeping quilt, mountain climbing gear. Making the jump to sewing *clothes* felt like a faraway goal, maybe for some more confident future self. After a lot of mulling (and making spreadsheets of skills and reading most of the sewing books in the library and looking at lots of blogs), I decided to give sewing my own clothes a dedicated try, a real one. I sewed some test garments and just let myself practice a while, and be okay with being bad and take my time with it.

I started getting together every few weeks with my friend Sarah, who works as an apparel designer, and our friend Katie to draft a collared shirt from scratch together, a process that made it all click for me. I loved it. I learned from adjusting parts of existing patterns and tracing patterns off of clothes I already had, then improving the fit or hacking them into something new. It just feels *so good* to wear pants with a few inch longer inseams and a higher rise and a waistband that fits. Having room to move in my shirts, lengthening the sleeves. Choosing beautiful fabrics, ones that are easy to wash and keep clean and that stand up to biking and walking and work in the studio. It feels good to be able to imagine something, then draw shapes on paper that make it. Such satisfaction and happiness, to know how to learn new skills, to get to talk about it all with friends who sew and like clothes.

Chapter 2

Get Your Workshop Set Up

what do you do in a sewing workshop?

You sew! That part's obvious. But you do lots of other stuff too, and that other stuff can help you think about how you might want to move in the space and what kind of space, furniture, and tools you might want or need (and what you already own that you can use). Besides sewing fabric, the things you will do the most are cutting and/or laying things out, and pressing with your iron. Because of this, your sewing workshop, wherever it is, will need three primary areas—a place for your sewing machine, a place for pressing, and a place for cutting. What form these three areas take is totally up to you and the physical space you have to work with.

where are you going to sew?

Though you might have an image in your mind of a spacious light-filled studio, it's much more likely you're dealing with part of a room that is also used for something else. There's definitely something to be said about dedicated space for sewing, where you can keep your sewing machine always set up and ready, but that's not possible in every life or every home. Realistically, think about where you are going to sew. Is there a room or a corner of a room you're not using? Is it well lit? A room you like to be in? You can sew very successfully on the kitchen table, and tuck your machine away at the end of the day. At the bare minimum, you'll need a table (any size) and a chair for sitting at your machine. You will also need a large flat surface for cutting, which can absolutely be a space you've cleared on the floor. Find space to set up an ironing board (or you could use a pressing mat or folded-up towel on the table next to your

machine for a smaller footprint) and you're ready to go. The most important thing is to get started and try sewing.

where we sew

AMY: Sewing takes up a decent amount of space in my life, so I let it take up a decent amount of space in my house—though it hasn't always been this way. Right now, the front room of my house (our former living room) is a flexible workspace–living space that includes my sewing desk and our dining room table. It's a somewhat weird arrangement, but it means that I can do my sewing work in a room with the best light in the house and be behind closed doors when needed without feeling like I'm shut away in a small dark corner of the house.

I like to set up my sewing desk (which is actually two secondhand wooden desks pushed together) in an L shape, with the sewing machine and a small self-healing cutting mat on one desk, and a small wool pressing mat, iron, and serger on the other. I use a swivel chair on wheels to switch between desks. Having these three essential stations all very close at hand—sewing, pressing, and edge-finishing—really helps me work efficiently. I keep essential tools on shelves under one of the desks, and on a tiered rolling cart. The rest of the sewing gear and my fabric stash is packed (not neatly) in a closet at the back of the house. The dining room table has many uses—a place for meals, for computer work, for piles of books, and for cutting fabric. All of this works for me right now, but I like to change things up as frequently as needed. A studio is a dynamic thing.

AMELIA: These days, I sew in our art studio, a ten-minute walk from our apartment, a small room with high ceilings and a huge window. It's so nice! An L-shaped table with my basic machine, the magnetic pincushion, snips and seam ripper and scissors all in reach. The ironing board and iron and pressing cloth and hams are there, also some

little drawers and boxes of other tools and machine feet, buttons, and elastics. I cut on the floor, or on the big print-shop table in the main room. I take great joy in the beauty of the little tools, the rainbows of thread, the stacks of fabric to use.

I've sewn in many places over the years: my mom's sewing room in the basement, then later, the sunroom porch. In Grandma Jo's sewing space, with the huge loom and big cutting table and the lake through the window. My college apartment where I'd screen-print something on fabric and turn it into bags or pillows. In the many small apartments Adam and I have shared, usually we stored the machine in a closet and brought it out for projects: quilts, bags, outdoors gear, pillowcases. That worked great! When I really started sewing my own clothes in earnest, and started working on pattern drafting, I gradually let it start to take up more space. I got a bigger cutting mat, an ironing board, a few more tools. Making a table for the sewing machine and letting work in progress remain out made it a lot easier to start, to keep going, to think: "I'll do just a bit," and then go where the momentum led.

sewing on the kitchen table, cutting on the floor

If your home doesn't allow for dedicated studio space, or if setting aside space just doesn't make sense for the way you want to sew, you can set up a temporary studio. This is super common; it's how we both started. Use your kitchen table or your desk. Put everything away after! Though you might be eager to set up a permanent spot, that's not always the best way to work. That said, once you get into it, you might decide to prioritize a small table or desk with the sewing machine on it, so it's easier to keep going with momentum.

Until then, maybe your sewing machine and other things are tucked in a corner or closet while not in use. You can use a rolling cart for your gear so you can easily stow it and pull it out. Stay organized as much as you can, and keep like things together. All the little moving parts you use for sewing can quickly become very chaotic—so even if it's a couple of ziplock bags in a cardboard box (or, better yet, a series of pouches you've sewn especially for holding sewing gear—project idea!) try to keep things together

and categorized. It's a lot easier to see if you have thread or a zipper that will work if they're all grouped with one another.

Cut on the floor! Unless you have a very large dedicated cutting table (which, though awesome, is rare), sometimes the floor really is the best option, no matter how fancy your home studio is. We cut on the floor all the time. You can really spread out your fabric as big as you need to and get all the way around it—but keep in mind that crouching down and working on the floor can be hard on the back and knees, so be mindful of your own body and what feels good for you. Sweep up a space and cut away!

what you definitely need

For any given project, you will need fabric and thread, and possibly other notions like buttons, zippers, elastic, or special kinds of thread, as indicated by the pattern. Here are the other things you will always want to have handy.

Sewing machine

We will go into our specific recommendations soon, but you for sure need a sewing machine. We say this because sometimes people ask us if our patterns can be hand-sewn. You can hand-sew clothes and bags if you want to—but you have to want to. It will take a long time, it isn't as simple as it sounds, and we aren't going to give you the specific instructions to set you up for hand-sewing success. The patterns in this book are geared toward machine sewing. It's worth it to own and learn how to use a sewing machine. (That said, hand-sewing is really lovely and fun, so it's worth trying out some embroidery or hand-quilting if you're curious.)

Things to cut with

The ideal scenario is to have two pairs of scissors: one for paper, one for fabric. The reason to have a pair of sharp scissors made specifically to cut fabric—and *only* fabric—is so that they'll cut accurately and without snarling the fabric or tiring your hands. If you use fabric scissors on paper, they'll dull quickly, but if you keep them just for fabric and continue to get them sharpened, a good pair of fabric scissors can last a lifetime. Sometimes called *dressmaking shears*, fabric scissors will move easily through fabrics and you will be glad to leave your paper scissors to their own happy life cutting paper. Amelia used a permanent marker to write FABRIC on the handle of her scissors, a handy thing to do if you have anyone else living with you who might accidentally use them for other things.

A rotary cutter is a tool with a little circular blade like a pizza cutter, which you roll across fabric to cut it. You use it along with a cutting mat and an acrylic quilting ruler. A cutting mat is essential if you're using a rotary cutter. They come in many sizes and are gridded, which helps with measuring. Amelia cuts out almost all of her garments and bags with a rotary cutter. Amy uses them for quilts but likes to cut garments with scissors. It's up to you; but since you will need fabric scissors either way, it can be good to

get started with fabric scissors and then try adding a rotary cutter later if you're drawn to it.

Seam ripper

A seam ripper is a special little cutter made to undo stitches that need to be undone. It can slice through a whole seam fairly quickly or cut individual stitches one by one. Use it, love it, embrace it. You will sew seams, you will rip seams—mistakes are part of the process. We use our seam rippers nearly every time we sew. Often one comes with a sewing machine, if you buy it new. It's good to have at least two on hand—they're usually inexpensive, and it's a bad feeling to be caught without a seam ripper when you need one.

Steam iron

You might already have an iron—great! As long as it gets hot and makes steam, it will be fantastic. If the steam function on your iron isn't working well (sometimes they get gunked up), or if you'd rather use a pressing mat on a tabletop, pressing spray such as a spray starch or sizing helps get things pressed and in place.

Ironing board or pressing mat

A traditional raised ironing board is great so you can stand up to press, and it gives you a large surface area to press on. It's designed for steam pressing, giving the steam somewhere to move through the fabric and the surface of the board.

A pressing mat is an awesome space-saving option. For a long while, Amy stopped using the steam in her iron and used a small pressing mat right on the wooden desk beside her sewing machine—in a small space this can be a really good option for helping your workflow feel natural.

Pins

There are lots of different lengths and thicknesses of pins, but the standard kind with a little glass or plastic ball at the top or all-metal straight pins will do just fine to start. Pinning is really helpful when you're learning to sew to keep things from shifting as you're sewing, and for some sewing tasks they're absolutely necessary, so you will want some on hand. It's nice to have some safety pins handy too.

Fabric-marking tools

To transfer patterns and markings onto fabric, you'll need a marking tool: Tailor's chalk is inexpensive and available

fabric scissors

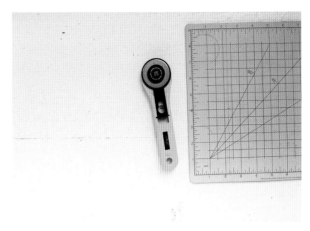

rotary cutter and cutting mat

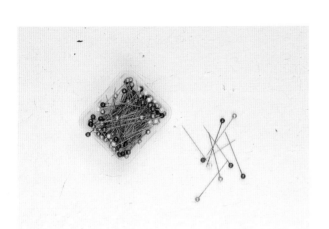

pins

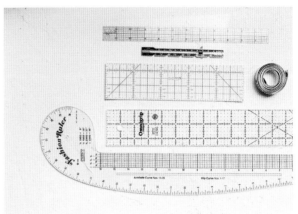

rulers and soft measuring tape

fabric-marking tools

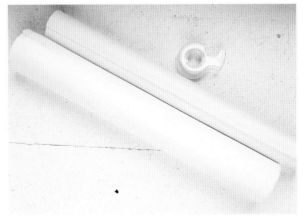

paper and tape

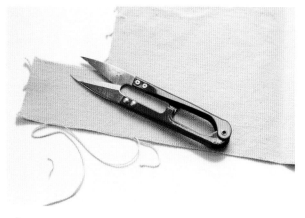

snips

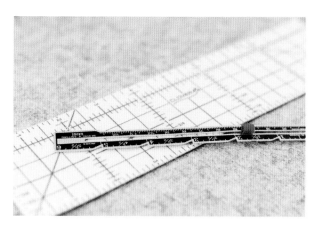

sewing gauge

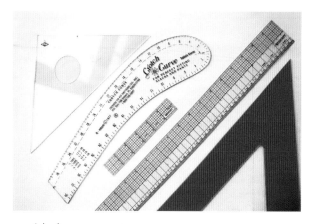

special rulers

pinking shears

clips

wax tracing paper and tracing wheel

in various forms intended for sewing, so that's what we'd recommend to start. There are also lots of other removable marking tools made for fabric. Try a few kinds to find what you like to use for different fabrics and tasks. Or don't buy anything yet, and use something you have on hand like pencil or permanent marker—they're nonremovable, but that can be okay to begin with.

Ruler and soft measuring tape

You need a soft measuring tape for taking your measurements accurately. In a pinch you can just use some string to find the length and then compare it to a yardstick (or meter stick), but measuring tapes are inexpensive and worth having. Some sort of ruler for making straight lines when you're tracing patterns is really useful too.

Paper, pencils, and tape

Gather a pencil and some paper, for tracing. You might have a few different kinds for different uses. For the patterns in this book use paper that is translucent enough to trace the patterns on to. Amelia uses a roll of tracing paper from a local art supply store. It's also nice to have butcher paper or a big roll of kraft paper for making more permanent paper pattern pieces, once you know you like the pattern and the fit adjustments you've figured out. And you will want some transparent tape (or whatever tape you have on hand) to use if you're hacking patterns from the book.

a more advanced tools list

Snips

These are little scissors used specifically for snipping thread. We *love* snips. It feels good to snip away all the little thread tails using little scissors especially suited for the task instead of trying to wave around your heavy fabric shears. They come in lots of different shapes and sizes, but our favorite kind are small metal ones with two sharp overlapping open blades that look like a hungry mouth waiting to eat your threads. Good to have multiple pairs of snips so you can keep them all over the place.

Sewing gauge

A sewing gauge is a really handy special ruler to have to measure folds for hems and seam allowances—this is one "extra" tool we think is worth having.

Special rulers

There are rulers of every shape and size—the sort of thing you can easily go wild with. You don't need all the different kinds, but a few are nice. A see-through, flexible grade ruler is really helpful for pattern hacks and general use. Though not at all necessary, you can go wild collecting fun rulers if you want to—we've been building our special ruler collections over the years with glee, and they do come in handy pretty often.

Pinking shears

Pinking is an alternate way to finish raw edges of fabric so they won't fray. Pinking shears cut the raw edges into a sweet little triangle pattern. Not strictly necessary, but good to have if you don't own a serger and don't want to zigzag stitch everything.

Clips

These are little plastic clips that almost look like hair clips that hold pieces of fabric together until you're ready to sew them. You can use sewing clips in place of pins, and they are really handy when working with thick canvas for bags. Amy likes them better than pins and uses them almost exclusively. They won't leave a mark in your fabric and can hold together fabric that is too thick for pins.

Wax tracing paper and tracing wheel

These two tools together are really useful, especially if you're making a lot of adjustments or hacks, or tracing things off existing garments. You put the paper down between your pattern and your second sheet of paper and then trace the lines with the tracing wheel, transferring a little line of dots onto your other paper. Amelia uses them all the time.

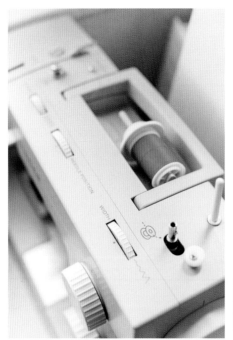

choosing a machine

You don't need 200 kinds of stitches, an internal computer, or really anything fancy on a sewing machine. If you're buying a sewing machine for the first time, look for simplicity, durability, and utility. Choose whichever machine is calling out to you. It's hard to go wrong unless you're buying something super complicated (which isn't bad, you will just likely not use many of the features), or something not built to last (steer clear of machines that are "mini," suspiciously inexpensive, or marketed to kids, for example). The stitches you will really need and use on your machine most of the time are straight stitch, backstitch, zigzag, and buttonhole. The rest are fun, but extra.

If you're looking for specific recommendations, we like to point people toward Brother CS6000i (Amelia's primary machine) and Singer Heavy Duty 4423 (Amy's secondary machine). Both of these machines can do everything you will need a machine to do. By the time you're reading this, there may be new versions of those, but that's the general idea. Amy primarily sews with a semi-industrial Juki TL-2000Qi, but it only sews straight stitch, so it's really mostly geared toward quilters or those who love the feel of industrial machines. These are the three machines shown in the photos in this book.

While it may be tempting to pick up a used sewing machine at the thrift store, it's usually not what we recommend. Used machines from unknown sources more often than not come with issues or *quirks* that are hard to resolve or just plain annoying. If your machine doesn't work well, you won't want to use it. That said, if a family member or a seller who seems trustworthy has an older machine that is still in great working condition, it's a good option to check out. Old machines can do some *amazing* sewing, and are often more sturdily built and easier to repair than modern machines.

serger: a special kind of sewing machine

A serger is another kind of sewing machine; it cuts and finishes the edges with a special loopy stitch. If you look at the inside of your ready-to-wear clothes, you'll see some serged edges. It can feel really satisfying and official to use one—but sergers certainly aren't necessary for making great clothes. If you're looking to buy one, we like to recommend the Juki MO-644D (pictured on page 190)—this is the one Amy uses and likes. Amelia uses a Pfaff Hobbylock 788 serger (shown above) that was her mom's—it's great, and there are a bunch of similar, sturdily manufactured sergers from the 1990s available secondhand. We recommend getting started with sewing for a while and then, if you get really into it, you can think about if you'd like a serger.

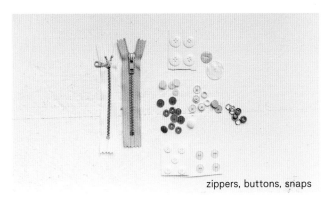

zippers, buttons, snaps

twill tape

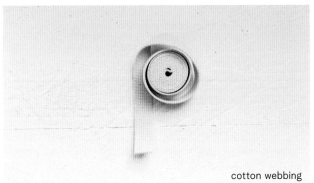

cotton webbing

elastic

what are notions?

Notions are all of the supplies you need for a sewing project that *aren't* fabric; this includes things like thread, zippers, elastic, buttons, and snaps. Small tools like snips or seam rippers are also considered notions, but we don't really mentally loop them into the category. We think of notions as *consumables*—things like bias binding or twill tape, which you use up as you sew.

At first, it's good to buy notions little by little as you need them. If you start to notice you're buying a lot of 1" (25 mm) wide elastic, for example, you can buy it in bulk to have on hand. Think of this a little bit like stocking your pantry—you always want certain staple foods at the ready for a quick dinner or snack. Same with notions—once you've found a rhythm with sewing and have figured out what kinds of things you like to sew, it's nice to have a sampling of seam bindings, elastics, zippers, and thread colors ready to go, so you don't have to make a dedicated shopping trip each time inspiration strikes.

a note on thread

There are lots of kinds of thread, but all-purpose will work fine for most projects. You can match your thread color to your project if you can swing it, but a close-enough match is good. We like to use thread with at least a little bit of polyester content for strength.

You will see other specialty threads that are more expensive, like cotton or silk. Cotton is mostly used for quilting and we avoid it for sewing clothes, unless it's something we plan to garment-dye after sewing. Some clothes look extra fancy with topstitching thread, and there is special button thread for hand-sewing buttons. You might want to use heavy-duty thread with stiff canvas. You will find your way to what you need, but all-purpose thread is great as you get started. For each color of thread, you will likely want to keep a matching bobbin wound. As you gather more spools of thread, you might want to get a box of spare bobbins that match your sewing machine—they're pretty inexpensive. You can keep thread in a box or drawer, and there are also special thread racks to organize them if you really get into it.

make it your own!

The best thing about setting up your workshop, whatever shape it takes, is adding the small touches and particularities that make it your own. Here are some details from our own workshops that we recommend:

- A small glass thread jar for all those little bits you snip off. It's fun to see the colors change from project to project.
- A little basket or box nearby for small fabric scraps.
- Baskets, trays, and drawers for notions storage.

- Pincushions are often adorable. Amelia has a lime green magnetic hedgehog pincushion, from a long-ago first visit to the Museum of Modern Art.
- A lamp for night sewing, to make sure you can see what you're doing.
- Artwork that inspires you. Amy has a half-finished quilt fragment hung above the worktable, and a little ceramic plaque that used to hang in her childhood kitchen growing up that says "Creative Minds are Seldom Tidy."
- A mirror for garment try-ons and adjustments.

Chapter 3

How a Garment Is Sewn, and Washed, and Worn

a top-of-the-mountain view

Let's talk about the putting-it-all-together part of sewing clothes. While the sewing itself does require some fine motor skills and coordination, new skills, and practice, the really tricky part is how to put stuff together, the order of operations. That's a spot where you could easily get discouraged or overwhelmed; You look at the pieces of your garment and just can't see it. Maybe you don't even start, or think sewing might be too hard. It *is* a bit of a weird puzzle.

The big-picture view is fundamentally the same across simple and complicated projects: once you've got the pieces cut out and all the supplies gathered, what you're doing is taking flat pieces of fabric and sewing them together, in a certain order, to make them into something useful. Here's what that looks like for the box top, for example:

1. Sew the back and front together along the shoulder seams.

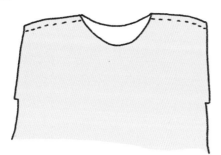

2. If you're adding sleeves, sew them in.

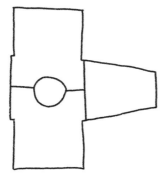

3. Sew up the sides of the garment, including the sleeves, if you have them.

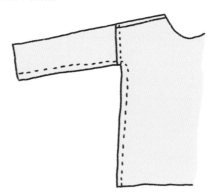

4. Bind the neck, and hem the armhole edges or sleeve openings and the bottom of the garment.

general order of operations for sewing garments

That same concept extends to most garments. First, you prepare any of the smaller parts that you will want to have on hand later, like pockets, belt loops, details, fly facings. Then, it's time to construct the main body of the garment—this might be shoulder and side seams on a top, or inseams and outseams on a pair of pants. Next, make any button plackets or bindings, like a neckline binding. Finally, finish the hems, like sleeve cuffs or the bottom of a shirt, and sew on any buttons. *The hem's always last*, that's the golden rule! It's good to know that pretty much any circumference type of sewing stuff is usually last.

After you're done sewing, you give the garment a last press all over, wash and dry it, and the project is complete. Of course this process can vary quite a bit. There are so many ways that work in sewing, so many methods for getting to the same place. Maybe you wait to put patch pockets on until after your garment is sewn up and you try it on, so you can get the exact placement. Then, the second time you sew the pattern you can put the patch pockets on while the fabric is flat, so it's easier to sew.

You will start to notice that there's a familiar flow to assembly, even across different things like tops and coats and pants. As complicated as something might look, it's just a lot of matching of two pieces of fabric together along the edge, sewing lines of stitches, and pressing—doing that again and again, one step at a time, until you've finished. If you're working with a pattern, you will likely have a book or booklet of sewing instructions to use, and you can follow those to learn how to put so many more complicated garments and bags together. It's really satisfying! Suddenly the weird puzzle feels possible to solve.

sewing and pressing

There's a joke that sewing is half pressing. It's true: you will get the best results if you press each seam or hem after each and every step, so you really do end up spending quite a bit of time pressing. If you're worried about sewing clothes that look home sewn, pressing is one of the key things that can make a garment look more like it is made professionally.

What is pressing, anyway? For sewing clothes there's a specific technique—you're not "ironing" like what you do when you're trying to get the wrinkles out of a button-down shirt before wearing it. You're really *pressing* down on a seam, with intent. Press the seam allowances open, then to the side. It flattens everything, helps you see and maintain the accuracy of your work, and reduces the bulk at the places where seams join. You're easing curves together, setting a seam neatly before you move on. Pressing helps snap everything into place and make a strong, long-lasting garment or bag. Just wanted to give you a heads-up, so you don't see it as this extraneous thing that's keeping you from "sewing" (aka making the stitches). Pressing is core to sewing. A big part of it! You and your iron are going to be *great* friends.

(Want to give it a try? We have some pressing practice on page 48.)

zigzag stitch

serging

pinking

bias binding

twill tape binding

french

clean finishing

Raw, unfinished fabric edges tend to unravel little by little over time, especially in the wash, and finishing is a practical way to make your garments last a long time. When pattern instructions say *"finish the edges,"* this is what they mean: You need to do something to the edges to keep them from fraying. It's important to clean finish all of the raw edges on the inside of your garment—finished seams are critical to making better, longer-lasting things. Longevity and beauty!

There are a few different ways to finish, some simpler than others:
- zigzag stitch (you can do this on most machines)
- serging (you need a serger to do this; see notes on page 29)
- pinking shears (slightly messy)
- binding (with bias tape or twill tape; see page 173)
- french seams (requires planning in advance, not suitable for all seams; see page 176)
- flat-felled seams (not pictured; see page 177)

And, of course, there are many more. It's totally up to you which finishing method to use—though sometimes a pattern will recommend a particular type of edge finishing, like French seams or bias binding, for that particular pattern. When you're beginning, finishing using a zigzag stitch (or serging, if you have a serger) is probably the easiest way, because it's less complex than thinking through all the steps of a French seam or flat-felled seam, and it's faster.

wash your garment so it becomes fully itself

Do you feel better about yourself after taking a shower? Clothes do too! Right after you sew a garment, it will often feel stiff and weird. Especially if it has a bound neckline or armholes, or darts, it might hang oddly and feel disappointing. Sometimes the seams need a chance to relax and settle after sewing. A quick run through the laundry helps that shift happen. We like to wash new garments we've sewn before really assessing our final opinion of them (glaring issues aside). Keep this in mind when you do the first try-on after it comes off the machine—it might seem a little strange at first, but wash it to see how it eases into itself.

learn from wearing

It's one thing to like the way a garment feels and looks when you're standing still in front of the mirror—it's another to still like it when you're moving through all the positions your body takes in a day. It's a good idea to wear-test a new garment to *really* see if it feels good to wear. Try raising your arms above your head, hugging yourself to pull your shoulders apart. Try squatting, bending down. Try sitting, reaching, and lying down. Cook dinner. Dance in the kitchen. Fold some laundry. Is there something bugging you? Is it too short, too long, too tight, too loose? You will know if it's not quite right, but it might take wearing rather than looking at it to realize the tweak that's needed. *A little more space here. A little more length there.* You will get a sense for it. These clothes are yours! And you have the power to make the tweaks you need to make, if not this time, then next time.

looking at clothes with new eyes

If you're the type of person who likes paying attention to how things work, how things are made, then there's a good chance you will really like sewing. When you look at clothes, before you start sewing, it might seem mysterious how they are made. Or maybe you've never given it much thought before. The first time you sew something it might be a small revelation: *Oh, that's it? That's it!* As you sew more, you will develop your intuition, and start to know how things probably go together *in a general sense.* You might even find yourself staring at clothing on strangers, puzzling out how you would make it. Imagining how the pattern pieces would look flat, how much fabric it might take. You might start looking more closely at seams and construction methods in the garments and bags you use all the time.

One day you will find that you can look at a garment and basically know how you'd go about constructing it. This makes sewing projects a lot easier over time—you spend less time with the instructions and can go faster, focusing more on fabric and fit. You'll start to see hacking possibilities as riffs on simple shapes, and dream up new ideas for how to sew yourself totally different looking clothes using the same patterns you've sewn before. All kinds of clothes will start to feel like something *possible* rather than mysterious.

how it all comes together

Think about making and eating good food. Maybe you try to make a new dish. The first time you try to cook it yourself, you follow the recipe closely, and maybe feel a little nervous that it won't taste good this time around. Once you finish it your confidence grows, but you have ideas about how you could make it taste even better. Maybe you use the basic ingredients or process of the recipe to make a totally new dish with different flavors. Maybe you use it as a jumping-off point for a whole new idea.

Like cooking, sewing can be slow and tedious when you're making something new to you, and easy and natural once you've practiced. It still takes a lot of thought and effort—but soon, in sewing, you will start to feel more like a chef instead of someone totally bound to the recipe. And *that* is a really good feeling.

Chapter 4

First Seams,
First Seam Rips

Lots of sewing is done in straight (or slightly curved) lines, so practice sewing some straight lines first, and using all the main functions on the sewing machine. Don't expect to be able to sew super accurately right away. Every sewing machine takes getting used to, especially if you're new to sewing altogether. No one needs to *ever* see these practice bits; this is just for you! The stakes are very, very low.

You will need a couple of squares of fabric—the sturdier, the better. Scraps of canvas or denim are ideal if you have some. But any simple woven fabric that isn't too shifty or slippery will be fine, even a worn-out garment or old sheet that you cut up.

If you're already pretty confident with a sewing machine—if you *aren't* new to sewing, or are returning after a while away—feel free to skip this chapter. But also a little practice never hurts!

hello, sewing machine

It's fairly common to get a sewing machine with excitement and lots of intentions and plans, but then feel a little intimidated about using it. Long instructions, many buttons! Or maybe your first attempt to make something wasn't as successful as you'd hoped, so the machine is sitting in a closet, unused, and pulling it back out again feels daunting. If these feelings ring true, don't worry, it's normal. The main way of getting to know your sewing machine is just using it to make things, and building skills over time.

It's worth just really *looking* at it to start. What can it do? What are the jobs of all the different parts? There are some functions that are common to all sewing machines (though they might have different names in your manual), and these are what you will want to familiarize yourself with the most. Look at your machine and see if you can find:
- handwheel
- stitch selector
- needle and needle plate below
- presser foot
- bobbin and bobbin case
- the threading path (the path from where you put the spool of thread, following through hooks and loops to, and through, the needle)
- on/off switch
- foot pedal

- reverse stitch lever or button
- tension dial

These things vary slightly from machine to machine, but they tend to be in similar spots and work similarly across machines. Once you learn how your sewing machine works—especially these parts—it should be pretty easy to sew on other sewing machines too. We recommend reading the manual and looking at online videos about your machine or similar ones, or asking a friend who sews to help you learn your way around your machine.

Before you start to sew, take some time to learn how to wind a bobbin and make sure your machine is fully threaded and ready to sew. Usually you want the top and bottom threads of your stitches to use the same thread, so you take an empty bobbin spool and put it on the bobbin winding part of the machine, and fill it up from the main spool. Most machines come ready to sew out of the box—so if you already have a bobbin with thread on it, feel free to use it to practice with, even if it doesn't match your thread. But sooner or later you will *have* to wind a new bobbin and rethread, so it's worth learning how ASAP.

Sewing machines also usually come with various extra feet—little metal or plastic swappable ends of the presser foot that help you do different things, like sewing buttonholes or zippers. You might try taking them on and off, and familiarizing yourself with what they can do. You can also take the needle out and swap it with a different one, which you will want to do occasionally if yours ever gets bent or broken or dull, or if you're sewing a specialty fabric (like silk or denim, so something very thick or heavy) that requires its own type of needle.

the threading path

tension dial

bobbin winder

handwheel

brother

CS-6000*i*
COMPUTER

stitch selector

reverse
stitch

00	01	02	03	04	05	06	07	08	09
10	11	12	13	14	15	16	17	18	19
20	21	22	23	24	25	26	27	28	29
30	31	32	33	34	35	36	37	38	39
40	41	42	43	44	45	46	47	48	49
50	51	52	53	54	55	56	57	58	59

presser foot
lever

needle

presser foot

needle plate

on/off switch
(on side)

bobbin and
bobbin case

how to sew a straight line

And now it's time to sew! If you can sew a straight line, you can sew anything. Grab a square-ish piece of scrap fabric; around 8" by 8" (20 by 20 cm) is ideal. Use a marking tool and a ruler to draw a quick maze onto it for yourself. Something like photos 1 and 2 below.

Now go to your sewing machine and put down your needle and presser foot at the beginning of the maze. Press down on the foot pedal to sew slowly, trying to sew your stitches as directly on the lines as you can. On most machines, how hard you press the pedal determines how quickly the machine sews, so start by pressing very gently. It might be easier to do this without shoes on.

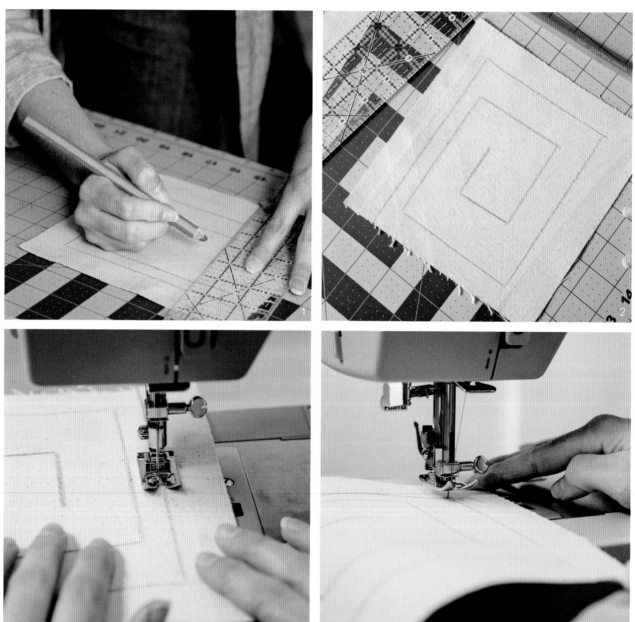

If you've never sewn on a sewing machine before, here's some advice: *Let the machine do the work!* The feed dogs (little grabby claws) under the fabric will pull the fabric under the needle for you, so you don't have to push it or pull it or anything. All you need to do is gently guide the fabric with your fingers and keep an eye on the spot that is *just about* to be sewn.

When you get close to a corner of the maze, sew extra slowly until you stop with the needle *down* in the corner. Now, keeping the needle down, lift the presser foot, and rotate the fabric until the next part of the maze is aligned so it is ready to go through the machine. (See image 4 on facing page.) This is a *pivot*. Put the presser foot back down and keep sewing.

You're really doing it now! Finish the maze! As you sew, experiment with speed. Practice your pivot. Work on accuracy, but also see that nothing "too bad" happens if you are a little bit imprecise for a while. YOU ARE SEWING! Hooray!

Do your stitches look weird? Sewing machine going wonky? Flip to page 50 for some troubleshooting.

- -

TIP! A quick note on the handwheel: Any time you're sewing and you need to be super precise, you can use the handwheel on the side of your machine instead of the foot pedal to go super slowly and really control the needle. Try it for the last few stitches as you approach a corner to pivot. It can help you hit the corner *just right*. Turn the handwheel in the same direction as it goes when you're sewing. (Generally this is toward you, counterclockwise if you're looking at the handwheel from the side of the machine.) You want to avoid turning it the "wrong" way, because going backwards might tangle the bobbin and needle threads underneath and cause thread jams.

- -

how to sew a seam

Now that you've sewn some straight lines on one layer of fabric, it's time to try a seam. Seams are the real building blocks of sewing: over and over, you're sewing pieces of fabric together—that's what making a seam is. Seams are typically sewn with the right sides of the fabric together. The right side is the one that you want to be on the outside of the garment, bag, etc. when you are finished sewing. In some fabrics it is very evident which is the right side. In this photo, the side with the dots is the *right side*, and the underside without the printed pattern is the *wrong side*.

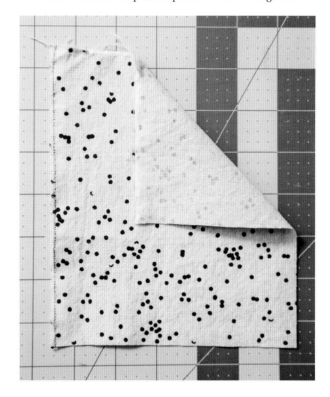

To sew a seam, you usually place your fabric pieces together with the right sides facing each other. Then, when you sew, you leave what's called a *seam allowance*: the space between the line of stitches and the edge of the fabric.

Seam allowances may change from pattern to pattern: Industrial sewing often uses 3/8" (1 cm), some sewing patterns oriented at sergers use 5/8" (15 mm), and pattern designers who work in metric have other standards. In the United States, 1/2" (13 mm) is pretty typical for home garment sewing, and also for most of the seams in this book.

Let's practice sewing with a 1/2" (13 mm) seam allowance. Depending on the machine, you might use the markings on the needle plate or markings on the foot to help you to guide the raw edges of the fabric along exactly 1/2" (13 mm) from the needle. Or put the needle down and grab a ruler to measure 1/2" (13 mm) to the right of the needle and mark the distance yourself with a piece of tape. You just need a visual reference so you can place the fabric edge correctly as you sew.

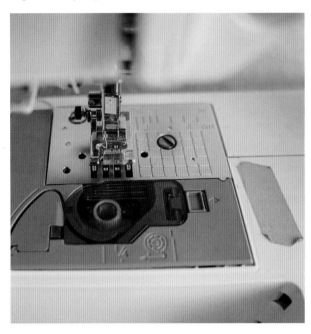

Grab another piece of fabric and cut it in half. Match up and layer the two pieces on top of each other with right sides together. No need to pin just yet.

Line up the edge of your layered fabric with the bottom of the presser foot and the seam allowance guideline, and gently press down on the foot pedal and begin to sew.

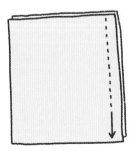

Slowly, slowly. Let the feed dogs pull the fabric through for you. Keep both hands on the fabric toward the front of the machine to guide it gently with your fingers. Do your best to keep the fabric edges aligned with the seam allowance guideline. You can keep your eyes on the fabric edge moving along the seam allowance guideline—the machine takes care of the rest. Don't try to watch the needle itself—it moves too fast. Sew until you reach the end of the fabric; then stop, lift the presser foot, and pull the fabric out. Cut the threads. You did it!

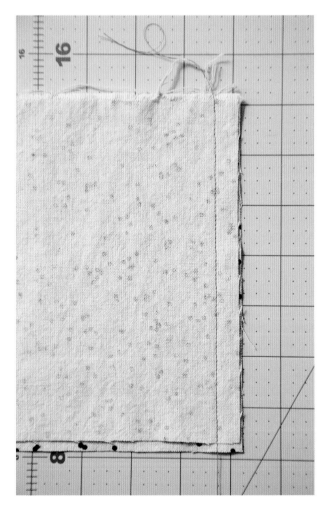

pin the middle

Now, try the same seam again, but pin the fabric first, before you sew. First, match up the pieces of fabric edges and pin near them through both layers, then pin in the middle between those two pins. Finally, place a pin in the middle of each gap between those. Place your pins perpendicular to the edge of the fabric.

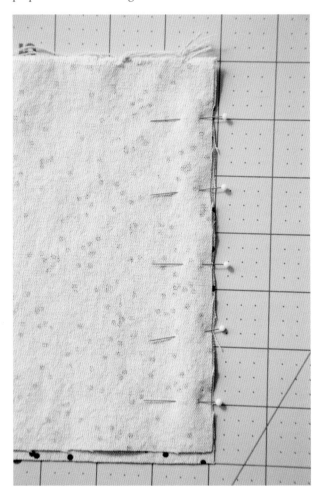

Now slowly sew the seam again, and as the presser foot approaches each pin, remove it—leaving pins in and sewing over them is potentially dangerous if your needle hits them, and it can also bend or break your needle. It's nice to have a pin box or magnetic pin holder close by the machine to deposit the pins in as you pull them out.

pin it to win it

How many pins you need depends on how long the seam is, and what your fabric is like, or if it's a curved or otherwise tricky seam. You will develop an intuition for it. Use as many pins as you want. As a beginner it's often easier to pin very generously, and as you get used to sewing you'll likely find yourself using fewer. As Amelia's friend Sarah says, "Pin it to win it!"

Some general advice for pinning: First, pin the two edges to be sewn, then any notches or seams you're trying to match up, and then pin the middle between where you placed pins. Then, if you need more pins, pin in the middle of those gaps. If you need to keep pinning, pin the middle of those four gaps.

Pinning at the start and end of a seam, and then in the middle, is better than the alternative, where you start by matching one end of the two pieces to be joined (like at the armpit of a box top) and then adding pins, one pin after another, until you get to the end (the hem, in our example). If you do it that way, the edges of the different pieces of fabric might not match up once you've gotten to the end of the seam.

- -
TIP! Sometimes it's nice to pin so the sharp point is closest to the raw edge, finding it easier to pull the pins out with the left hand as you sew. Try it and see what you like.
- -

backstitching

Take a look at that seam you just made. If you try to pull apart the two layers of fabric at the top or bottom of the seam with your fingers, even very gently, you can probably start to undo the stitches. Oh no, that isn't what you want!

Backstitching is how you keep the stitches at the beginning and the end of a seam from coming apart. Start sewing forward at the beginning of the seam, sew just a few stitches (approximately two to four—but you don't have to carefully count or anything), and then use the reverse stitch lever or button on your machine to go back over the stitches you just made in the opposite direction. You usually have to hold down the lever or the button for as long as you want the machine to go in reverse, while pressing down on the foot pedal.

Sew backwards on top of those same two or four stitches you started with, then release the reverse stitch lever/button to sew forward again, and keep sewing as usual. While you're learning, you may want to stop sewing, press and hold the backstitch button or move the lever, then press the foot pedal again—three separate steps, until you get used to the feel of it all. Once you've gotten used to it, you'll find yourself doing this all as one quick motion.

Let's practice. Grab a scrap piece of fabric and practice using your reverse stitch lever/button, going forward and back as much as you want. What does your machine feel like when it's going backwards? Try it:

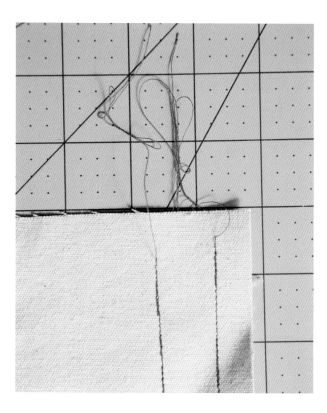

Hooray! Take a look at the seam you just made—if you try to pull apart the top and the bottom you probably can't really get it undone. Superstrong seams!

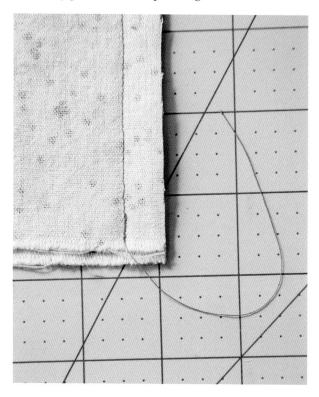

Once you've gotten the hang of reversing your machine to backstitch, try it out at the beginning and end of a seam. You'll do a lot of this when you sew clothes and bags.

Cut another piece of fabric in half and align the pieces with right sides together (pin if you want) for another seam. Starting at the top edge, sew a few stitches, backstitch, then keep sewing down the seam until you get to the bottom, backstitch again, and then sew back down to the end. You're aiming for something like this, where you backstitch at the beginning and end of the seam you're making.

Note: Backstitching is not shown in diagrams in this book, or in the instructions. Always backstitch at the beginning and end of every seam, unless otherwise instructed.

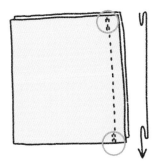

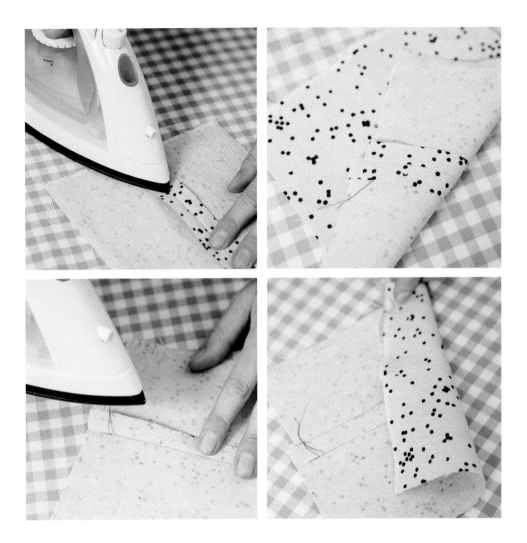

how to press,
the sewing way

Pressing is a huge part of sewing. Committing to carefully pressing your seams every step of the way through a project is a great way to achieve a beautiful result. You might feel tempted to skip the steps that involve an iron, or wait to press everything all at once at the end—don't! Take the time to press as you go and you will see the results in your project.

The primary reason irons are used in sewing is to set and guide the seams to help them all work together. Use your iron to "press" the seams, which is exactly how it sounds. Instead of simply wiggling the iron around, as you would if you were trying to get the wrinkles out of a shirt, press the iron straight down on the seam with gentle force, helping train the fabric to stay where you want it. Any time a pattern's instructions tell you to press, this technique is what they mean.

Grab that seam you just made, with the backstitching at the top and the bottom. Take it over to your iron and practice pressing the seam allowance open.

A pattern will often have specific directions when it comes to *how* to press the seams—it may tell you to press them both together in a certain direction, especially if your edges are finished. Try pressing both seam allowances to one side also.

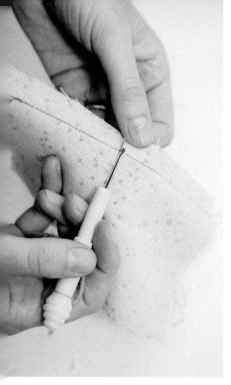
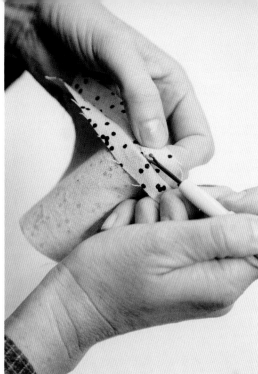
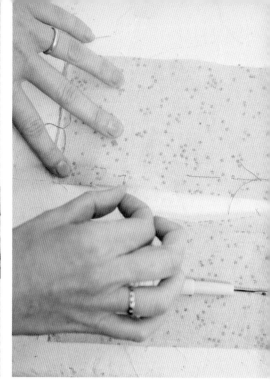

seam ripping!
hooray!

No matter how long you've been sewing, you *will* use the seam ripper because you *will* make mistakes—small ones *and* big ones. Frequently! During a sewing project, there are lots of reasons that you might seam rip. Some are:

- sewing with incorrect sides of the fabric together
- joining incorrect pieces together
- using a wrong seam allowance
- making stitches that aren't straight or even
- stitches that look terrible because the tension is wonky

It's much easier to fix in the moment than to try to fix it later, so if you see an imperfection you think will bother you later, just go ahead and seam-rip and redo it.

One way is to go stitch by stitch on the *outside* of the seam, sliding the sharp part of the seam ripper under each little line of thread. Often once you rip a few of the stitches in a seam you can pull out a few inches (or centimeters) of thread at a time.

Or seam-rip by opening up the seam allowance and wiggling the tip of the seam ripper down between the pieces of fabric, then rip the whole seam in one go. Careful though—if things go askew and you accidentally rip a little hole in your fabric it's not easy to repair. Move slowly and carefully.

To practice, go ahead and try to rip out one of the seams you just made and pressed. Seam ripping can be frustrating, but it's also simple and oddly meditative. Sometimes it's nice to do while watching a show or a movie, or listening to the radio, or having a chat. Seam ripping is sort of its own art, with finesse and techniques. You will get *plenty* of practice as you sew your first garments and bags.

finishing

Now it's time to practice finishing. Turn back to page 37 and choose one of the finishing options. The simplest one with a regular sewing machine is the zigzag stitch. Set your machine to zigzag stitch (try it with a 2.5 mm length, and a 3-3.5 mm width). Line a piece of fabric up under your presser foot and sew a line of zigzags along the raw edge of the seam allowance to keep the edge from unraveling. Depending on what the pattern indicates, sometimes you will finish each seam allowance separately, and sometimes you will finish both together. Try it out: Sew two pieces of fabric together to make a seam, then zigzag along the edge to finish both edges of the seam allowance together. It will look like this:

stitches and their uses, and the different feet

We've mostly been using the stitch that the machine makes when it turns on—for most machines, that's a 2.5 mm-long stitch. That's the stitch you will use most, but your machine probably has a bunch of other stitches, and they're used for different things.

You can make a stitch sampler! This is a great way to check out all that your machine can do. Grab one of your scrap pieces of fabric and play around with a bunch of the stitches on your machine. Experiment with the various settings for widths and lengths. If you find a stitch or setting you particularly like, write down the details to possibly use later. You might flip open your sewing machine's manual (or google for a PDF of the manual online if you don't have a paper copy) and try figuring out how to use any special feet for special stitches like the buttonhole or blind hem. Playing around helps keep them from being a scary mystery.

you probably won't break it

You might feel nervous approaching the machine, worried about messing something up. An encouragement—*you probably won't break it!* Sewing machines are very sturdy, and made to be used. Even if something does go a little wrong, it's almost always possible to fix. Approach your machine with confidence and calm. And if something does seem weird, the internet is there to help. It's silly, but it's true. Most seemingly insurmountable problems we've had were remedied by a little bit of research. At the very most extreme, you can replace a part and/or contact a professional.

why isn't it working?

Even though you probably won't break it, inevitably there will be times when things will go wrong or feel bad or weird. Here are some things that can happen when you're using a sewing machine, and what you can do about them:

- You might break or bend a needle. It's okay, just put in a new one. That's why your machine comes with several, and you can always buy more. Even if there's nothing visibly wrong with your needle, sometimes switching to a fresh one can make a difference, especially if it's been awhile.
- Your thread might jam! Unjam it, rethread the entire thread path and/or bobbin section, and nine times out of ten that fixes the issue.
- Your tension might be a little wonky. Rethread, change your needle, or fiddle with the tension dial and do some test stitches for a while.
- There could be something weird going on with your bobbin. Take it out, make sure the thread is wound tightly and evenly—that it isn't all bumpy or loose.
- Your machine might suddenly make a loud, alarming noise! Feels scary—but what's going wrong probably isn't as bad as it sounds. Take the noise as a sign to *stop sewing*, carefully see what's going on (often thread jams cause these noises), and go from there.
- Your machine might need some cleaning and care. Take a few minutes to sweep out all the collected dust and lint (soft paintbrushes work great for this!) and lightly oil the machine's mechanical moving parts (your machine may come with a small container of oil).

If you aren't sure what to do, this works like 80% of the time: Fully unthread the top thread and guide it through the full threading path. Especially make sure the thread is fully in place between the tension dials (lifting your presser foot separates the tension dials), and check that it goes through all the little hooks and guides on the threading path in the right order. Next, take the bobbin out of the bobbin case and rethread it too. Try sewing again. A lot of machines have detailed threading diagrams in the manual, or you can watch a video online if you need help.

personal vs. perfect

Sewing takes practice, and everyone learns differently. You may not be able to sew as precisely as you want to right away. You might feel frustrated in the early days of sewing clothes if you're a person who really likes things super tidy and precise. Take your time, be gentle with yourself, and you will slowly gain confidence and move closer to your goal. We bet you'll love and be proud of some of your early more imperfect projects too, even if just because they're yours.

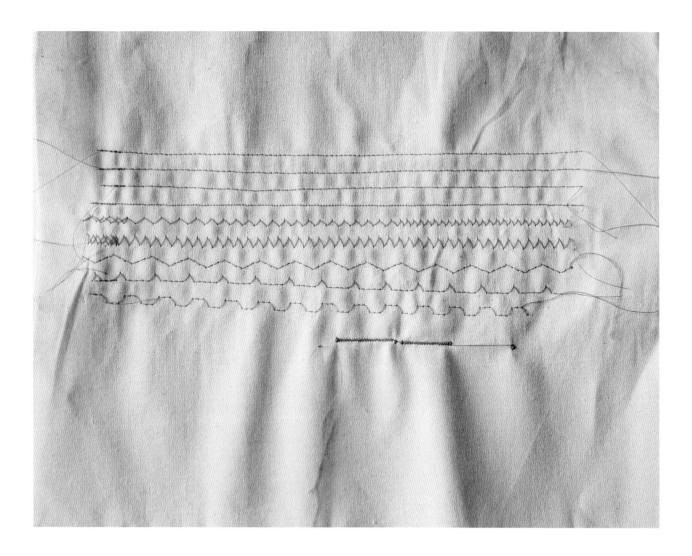

Chapter 5

It's All About the Fabric

The sewing is important in a sewing project, but the fabric is equally important. You can sew something flawlessly, but if you're dissatisfied with the fabric, you probably won't love what you've made. Fabric selection is nuanced and personal—sort of an art form in itself.

against overwhelm

We won't understate it: It is really, really easy to become overwhelmed by fabric. Especially if you're just venturing out, it is difficult to know where to start and what to buy. This chapter can be a launching pad to help you get started. You will soon develop a personal taste in fabric and find fabric you love that will become your favorite clothes.

A good place to start is with any favorite garments in your closet. Look at the tags to find the fabric's fiber content. Hold the fabric between your fingers. Think about the weight: Is it light like a thin silk scarf? Heavy like nonstretch denim? Is it solid, yarn-dyed, screen-printed? Woven or knit? Stretchy or not? What colors? Take note of some of the characteristics of the fabrics you like best, and when you set out to buy fabrics, look for those things.

drape, weight, ease

Drape, weight, and ease are the three variables you can tweak to get the fit you want. Every fabric is unique in the way it wears, a special mixture of drape and weight. *Ease* is a way to manipulate the space between your body and the clothing. *Drape* is the way the fabric falls. Fabric might be flowy or stiff—two sides of the drape spectrum. *Weight* is how heavy or light the fabric is—literally and figuratively. We say *literally* because often fabric is actually classified by its weight in ounces per square yard (oz/yd²) or grams per square meter (gsm). A 12 oz/yd² (407 gsm) cotton denim is heavy, where a 3 oz/yd² (102 gsm) cotton lawn is light. Weight and drape *usually* go hand in hand, with heavier fabrics generally having less drape, or being stiffer, though there are exceptions.

Ease refers to the amount of space between your body and your clothing. For example, a skintight leotard would have very little ease (little to no space between your body and the fabric), whereas voluminous pajama pants would have quite a lot of ease (lots of space between your body and the fabric). Drape and weight affect the way the ease feels to wear. Those pajama pants in stiff, heavy fabric would almost stand up on their own, far away from your body, whereas pajama pants in flowy, light fabric would fall closer to your body for a different fit entirely.

It takes experimentation to fine-tune your use of these three variables, but learning to use weight, drape, and ease to your advantage, strategically and thoughtfully, is really the *key* to a satisfying garment.

a taxonomy of fabrics

These are the different characteristics you will choose between when you look for fabrics:

- *fiber content*: cotton, linen, wool, silk, rayon and other synthetics, everything else
- *construction/structure*: woven (usually nonstretch) vs. knit (often stretchy, requires different sewing techniques and tools). All the projects in this book are intended for woven fabrics.
- *weight*: light (silk, cotton lawn), medium (woven cotton, silk noil, linen), heavyweight/bottomweight (most denim, canvas)

These characteristics all work together to determine how the fabric feels and acts as you're sewing or wearing it. Sometimes you might hear this called *hand*: drape, softness, flexibility, compressibility, or density. You could say a woven cotton fabric has a dry, stiff hand, whereas a silk charmeuse might have a smooth, soft hand with high (flowy) drape. *Hand* helps you describe a fabric to yourself: two cotton canvas fabrics of the same weight can have a really different hand, a different feeling that could make you prefer one to the other.

fabric parts and terms

Right side and wrong side

The terms "right side" and "wrong side" are used in sewing to indicate which side of the fabric will be on the outside (right side) or inside (wrong side) of the finished project. Some fabrics have a very obvious right side and wrong side; the right side is the more vibrant and obvious top of the fabric, and the wrong side, the back, is often more subtle or faded. Many apparel fabrics do not have an obvious right side or wrong side.

Selvage

Woven fabric is produced on a loom, and the selvage edges are the sides that are finished and don't unravel: That's where the weft threads loop back at the edges of woven fabric (and some knits too). If you've gotten fabric cut off of a bolt or roll, the selvages are the two sides that haven't been cut by scissors.

Grain

It's important that woven fabric is cut on the grain, meaning that you need to align pattern lines with the natural grainline of the fabric when you cut the pieces out, to prevent misshapenness or stretching. Take a close look at your fabric. You will see threads that run straight vertically and horizontally, the warp and weft. These threads form the straight grain and crosswise grain of the fabric. Sometimes the straight grain (parallel to the selvage) is just called "the grain," since it's the most commonly referenced one.

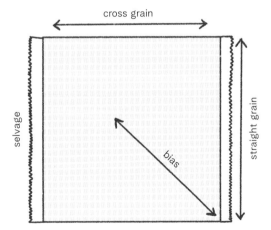

fabric grain, and why it's important

Have you ever worn tops that hang weirdly, or pants with legs that inexplicably twist toward the calves no matter what you do? Many mysterious disaster garments (likely including some you've bought from the store) can be explained by a bad match of the pattern pieces to the fabric grain. You can avoid this by paying attention to the straight grain of the fabric at two important times:

1. When you lay the fabric out flat to prepare it to cut out pattern pieces.
2. When you're laying the pattern pieces on the fabric before cutting them out.

Most pattern pieces have a grainline marked on them, showing you how to line up the pattern pieces with the straight grain of the fabric, typically with the grainline arrow parallel to the selvage edge. (Lots on how to do this in Chapter 6 on page 69.) It's really super important to align your pattern pieces on the indicated grain when you're sewing clothes and bags: This gives the right fit and drape, and keeps all the parts of the garment growing and shrinking with wear and laundering at the same pace. You can really see why when you try to pull the fabric either vertically or horizontally: You should notice that the fabric doesn't have much stretch or give at all. By comparison, if you tug on your fabric diagonally from two corners, you will notice quite a bit of stretch—this direction is called the *bias*.

where to get it

The best place to start shopping for fabric is your local small fabric shop. Find out if there is one near you. It's really hard to buy fabric online in general—but especially as you're getting started, when you don't know yet what you like or what you're looking for. It helps to shop somewhere where you can touch everything and find great customer service, so you feel supported and excited and ready to go. (Plus, a local sewing shop is a great place to scope out the other sewists in your area and find out if there are any meetups, classes, or events. Lots of friends to be made.)

If you don't have a local fabric shop, your journey toward sewing will just be a tiny bit trickier. There are a lot

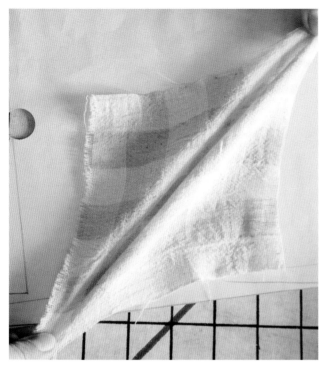

of amazing fabrics available online, but they're . . . online. You won't be able to touch them to see if you've found what you really want, and fabric websites differ widely in how much detail they include about fabric weight and drape. But don't be deterred. If you have to shop online, there are great places to do it. A lot of great small business fabric shops have online stores, so you can still shop small even from afar.

You can also go to a big chain fabric store. We've often been disappointed with the quality of the fabrics there (and their treatment of workers, and their politics), but every so often we find a fabric that we really love, and big chain stores can be a convenient and accessible option. Look for natural fibers and a nice drape, and don't be afraid to ask questions at bigger stores too.

There are also specialty fabric stores, like special shops for outdoor fabrics, ones that sell only leather or denim, and various Etsy fabric boutiques. If you're looking for something unusual and struggling to find what you want in a traditional fabric store, it's worth checking to see if there's a supplier that specializes in what you want. They will often have more choices and better customer service for that kind of fabric anyway.

Though sourcing new fabric means that you can usually find exactly what you're looking for, most of the time we really like to find fabric secondhand and use what we already have. Secondhand fabric is the most sustainable (and often cheapest!) way to source fabric for sewing. For lots of thoughts about sustainable and secondhand fabric sourcing, flip over to Chapter 23.

investigate!

Touch the fabric! Touch it all! Shop in person for fabric as much as possible, especially in the beginning, while you're learning what you're looking for. Feel it between your fingers, unroll it and see how it drapes and moves. Ask questions. If you can, try looking at the fabric next to a window or in natural light, as some tones can really look different in different lighting. When you hold a piece of fabric, what type of garment does it seem like it's asking to be made into? A personal investigation of fabric is the way to start.

fabric types, applied

Here are some fabrics matched with things we might want to make—a personal fabric investigation applied. You can make the same kind of thing yourself, maybe as a little list in a notebook to start, adding in some swatches and sketches if you'd like.

tops
- silk noil for a luxuriously soft and drapey woven t-shirt
- linen for an easy summer tank
- drapey woven cotton for a lightweight long-sleeve layer

bottoms
- denim pants
- lightweight woven cotton balloon pants
- linen ankle-length skirt

dresses
- silk box dress for something luxurious
- woven cotton ruffle dress
- linen box dress for summertime

bags
- big tote made out of a canvas drop cloth
- small zip pouch out of quilted fabric
- mesh drawstring bag for swimming gear

wear the colors and prints and stripes you are drawn to

There are lots of fabrics out there, in every possible color, texture, and print. More than you would find in a clothes store. If you like color, if you like prints, if you like a particular type of fabric or you want all of your clothes to be a certain palette of blues or a bright poppy pink—SEWING IS GOING TO BE AWESOME FOR YOU! However you want your handmade wardrobe to look, it doesn't need to look like anyone else's. The fabric to make it happen is out there waiting for you. Choosiness and discretion are worth it here. You might be tempted to think, "Okay, the color's not great, but I'm still going to buy it." But if it's not bringing you that joy, you're most likely not going to wear it—at least not past the initial novelty of having made it. Find the fabrics that you're drawn to!

surface design

There are even more ways to customize your fabric beyond what you can buy. Here are some quick ideas—we won't go into great detail about these here (there are whole books about these techniques), so research anything that piques your interest.

- dyeing
- block printing
- screen-printing
- fabric painting
- digital fabric printing
- embroidery
- appliqué

Surface design can be a way to bring more art-making into the process of sewing, to flesh out your most personal ideas.

spending money on fabric

You will spend money, but it's up to you how much. Making a sewing budget for your projects, even a loose one, is a good idea. You can give yourself a budget and a goal for how many projects to make using that budget. Then, you can approach buying fabric and notions and patterns with an idea in mind of where you can choose the more expensive fabric and where you might want to do some creative secondhand sourcing. Keeping track of how much you intend to spend and how much things cost can help with the chaotic feeling that can come from haphazardly taking on new projects and buying new fabric willy-nilly (which we've done plenty of).

start easy

Some fabrics are easier to work with than others. As you are learning to sew, start with fabric that is going to work with you rather than against you. If you've never sewn a top before, don't start with chiffon, or something so fussy you can't keep it together. It's a skill in itself to work with a harder fabric like silk, so it's smart to learn garment sewing basics first, then learn to work with more difficult fabrics.

Imagine what it will be like to cut and sew the fabric you're considering: Will it hold its structure, is it not too slippery, can you see the grain? Your instincts are probably right: If you notice a tinge of worry that a fabric might be too tricky to sew with right away, listen to that—go for easy! If you want a specific recommendation, we'd say a mid-weight woven cotton or cotton blend without too much texture is a good place to start.

really, it's all about the fabric

We have to say it clearly: The clothes you make will only be as good as the fabric you make them from. This sounds like something that could be discouraging, but it doesn't have to be. It just means you have to get as excited about the "choosing fabric" step as you are the "sitting down to sew" step. It means that *the fabric itself really matters.* We wrote this chapter at such length and detail because no one really ever told us this stuff when we were learning

to sew. Thinking it through then might have helped us make things we really liked earlier.

It can be really hard to find good fabrics: We think sourcing fabrics is one of the biggest barriers to sewing clothes at home. Often buying good fabric new will be just as expensive as buying a brand-new garment from the store. (Fast fashion sets unrealistic expectations.) And hunting for nice fabric secondhand takes a lot of time and dedication. If you find fabric you're excited about, all the time and investment of sewing clothes becomes more worth it.

Aim for fabric you really like to touch, fabric that reminds you of your favorite clothes. Look for it in places that make you feel good. Once you find your fabric, use it to make beautiful, simple, long-lasting clothes that will help the fabric (and ultimately the way *you feel*) shine. This is an invitation to chase after something soft and beautiful and wear it on your body.

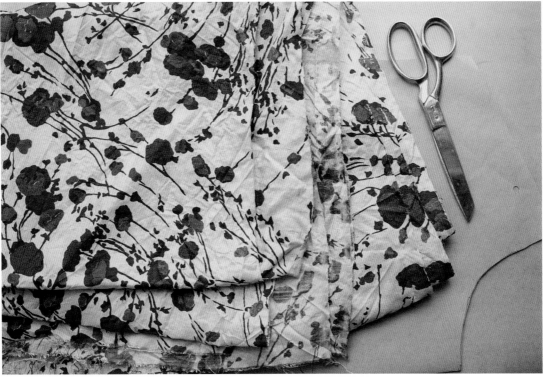

Chapter 6

How to Begin

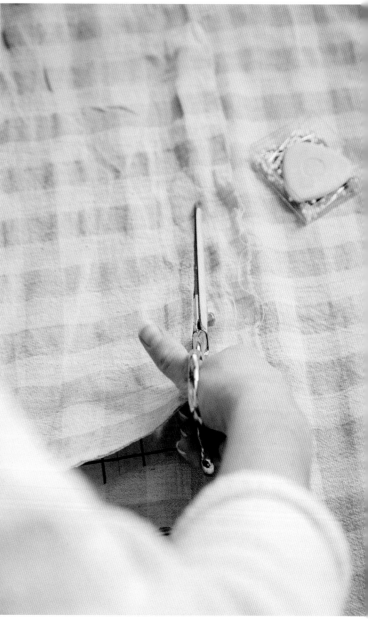

In a lot of ways, sewing is a series of many small decisions peppered with bursts of action. As much as you might imagine "sewing" as just *sitting at the table at your sewing machine, making the stitches,* there's a lot to do before you get to that point. And what you do before almost entirely determines how your project will turn out. It's super important. And it's a lot of work! We'll lay it all out for you here.

a helpful prep checklist

You might not do *all* these steps, or you might do them in a different order, but this is the general path through:

- ☐ Choose your project.
- ☐ Measure yourself, so you have your current body measurements handy.
- ☐ Use the pattern's measurement chart to choose which size(s) you will use and which version (sometimes called a *view*) you will make. (Look at the measurement chart before you buy the pattern.)
- ☐ Get the pattern ready. (Buy it, download it, print it, tape it together, etc.)
- ☐ Get the pattern laid out and look at all the pieces; take inventory.
- ☐ Trace copies of the pattern pieces you want to use in your size(s), or just cut them out. Make adjustments to the pattern pieces, grade between sizes if you need to (more on this later), and otherwise customize.
- ☐ Hack the pattern pieces into something new if you want.
- ☐ Gather fabric and notions.
- ☐ Prepare your fabric.
- ☐ *Optional:* Make a test garment.
- ☐ Read through the sewing instructions.
- ☐ Get ready to cut. (Iron any wrinkles out of your fabric, lay out the fabric, align the grain.)
- ☐ Arrange the pattern pieces on the fabric.
- ☐ Take a deep breath, then cut the pieces out.
- ☐ *Sew, sew, sew!*

choosing your project

There are *so many* patterns out there that it can be difficult to choose what you want to make. We won't go into all of the different places to find sewing patterns here, but just repeat what we have been saying all along—look to your closet for what kinds of clothes and bags you love, find what you're drawn to, start simple (unless you really want to sink your teeth into "complicated"), and then enjoy the process.

If you're choosing your first project ever (yay!), we recommend you look for a pattern with three general characteristics:

- simple (patterns marked "beginner-friendly"!)
- not a ton of fabric required (lower stakes, easier to handle!)
- something you're excited to use (like something to wear in a color you love!)

Beyond those three suggestions, the sky's the limit! This book has some great options for first projects: If you want to begin with a garment, try the box top (Chapter 7). If you want to start with a bag, try some simple pouches (Chapter 15). Most of all, just pick something and dive in!

how to measure yourself

For sewing clothes, taking your current body measurements is a good way to start each new project. Wear your underwear only, or form-fitting clothes, so your measurements are accurate. Grab a soft measuring tape and a notepad and head over to a mirror. Use the mirror to get the tape fairly straight and level all the way around your body, not drooping in the back or pinching in. Here are some common measurements that come up in this book:

BUST: Measure around your bust/chest at the widest part, usually right over your nipples.

HIGH BUST: This measurement is useful for people with breasts. Measure around your body right under your armpits where your chest is more flat just above where your bust begins to curve.

WAIST: Measure around the point where your body naturally hinges when you bend side to side, usually a bit above the belly button.

HIPS: Measure around the widest part of your hips and butt. This might be a bit lower down than you expect. Make sure the tape measure is parallel with the floor all around.

Jot your measurements down on a sheet of paper, on the pattern itself, or in your sewing notebook (see Chapter 20 about sewing notebooks), and add the date. Round to the nearest 1/8" (3 mm)—size charts won't be that precise, but having a more exact number can help you decide on sizing.

reading a pattern size chart

Once you have your measurements, you can use the pattern's measurement chart to choose which size you want to make. Use your body measurements, the recommended measurements listed for each size, and the finished garment measurements to help you decide what size to trace, or which sizes to trace between (called *grading*, more on that soon).

size charts are arbitrary, it's all about the ease

The secret of size charts is that they are by nature quite arbitrary. There is no one standardized set of measurements that everyone uses to correspond to particular sizes, and even if there were, each body is uniquely shaped. You will likely find that your measurements don't fit you perfectly into one size. Likewise, the way we like our clothes to fit is extremely personal.

Ease is central to the process of finding or making clothes you really love. You already have intuitive opinions about ease, whether you call it that or not. You know your favorite sweater? Or the t-shirt that feels perfect? When you love how something fits you, what you really love is the garment's *ease*—the unique fusion of the fabric's weight and the amount of space between your body and the fabric underneath your clothes—the way it hangs on you.

Ease is built into sewing patterns, and into all clothes. You need a minimum amount of ease so you can wear the garment—so you can fit into it and still move—and then there's almost always more added for style. For every pattern, the designer has an intended fit in mind, and they have devised their size chart accordingly, recommending a certain size for certain body measurements. To figure out how much ease is built into the garment by the designer, compare finished garment measurements for the size recommended to you (if provided) with your body measurements. If you're having trouble visualizing what a certain amount of ease would look like in context, you can measure the ease of some of your favorite clothes for a reference point.

what if I'm between sizes?

If you're between sizes, or right on the border, how you respond depends on where you fall in the measurement chart and the type of garment. You can choose to go up or down a size, depending on whether you'd prefer a more snug or looser fit. The more ease you choose, the more roominess you'll have. For a more fitted garment, you might want to *grade between sizes*. That means that when you are tracing your pattern pieces, you start with the pattern line for one size (for example, at the bust/chest) and then draw a smooth line out to a *different* size (for example, at the hips) to connect them together, making your pattern piece out of a blend of the two sizes that match your measurements.

get the pattern ready

Pull out the patterns from the back of the book and take a look at them now. You might want to use an iron with the steam off to press out any creases in the paper. With other patterns, you will either be using a printed pattern with a large pattern sheet you can trace or cut your size from, or a downloaded print-at-home PDF file that you will print on regular paper and tile together kind of like a puzzle. (More on page 188.)

a pattern inventory

Look for a small diagram somewhere on the pattern envelope or in the instructions that gives an inventory of the pattern pieces. For the box top pattern in this book, it's simple: just two (very similar) pieces, a front body and a back body.

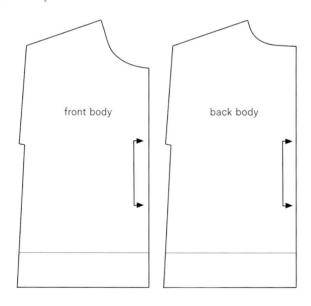

front body   back body

As you get into more complicated garments, like pants with a fly front, you might have a dozen or more pattern pieces. Or a pattern might have different "views" or style options, and you will only need some of the pattern pieces; which ones you use depends on which variation you're making. A bag pattern offers several different sizes, and you need to pick which you want. That's what the pattern inventory is for—a map to show you the possibilities.

how to trace and use the patterns in this book

This book's pattern sheets are printed front and back with overlapping pieces, so you need to trace the pattern pieces you need instead of cutting them out. Place tracing paper on top of the pattern and copy each piece you need, working slowly, using a ruler and a sharp pencil or dark fine pen. Transfer any markings like grainlines, fold marks, notches, and darts. You might be making adjustments to the pattern, like grading between sizes or lengthening or shortening pieces as you trace them, too.

Add a quick label with the garment name, piece name, and cutting instructions to each traced pattern piece so you know what they are when you come back to sew again. Once you have all the pieces traced, cut them out right along the lines you drew.

adjusting the pattern

It can be intimidating to change the pattern. *What if I mess it up? What if it gets all wonky and weird?* Those are valid questions. But sometimes making small (or big) adjustments is exactly what you need to take a garment from "just fine" to "really great." And, as with your sewing machine, you probably won't break it!

Some adjustments are simple and are typically done before you even make your test garment; others you will make after you make a test garment. You might realize, for example, that you are often finding you need to make things longer, so you will come to anticipate this when you're approaching a new pattern and will make the adjustment right away before ever cutting any fabric. Amelia usually adds several inches in length to the inseam of pant legs, for example, and grades a size or two between the hip and waist.

It might feel frustrating to need to make adjustments to a pattern. It's *normal.* Patterns are drafted to fit a lot of bodies well, but very few bodies perfectly, and there are natural limitations. It's similar to trying on clothes at the store—all of those clothes have a size chart too. Being able to make adjustments to a sewing pattern is one of the most awesome things about sewing clothes, in our opinion. It takes some experimentation and learning, sure, but once you figure out some simple and subtle ways to make your clothes *really* feel good to wear instead of *almost,* you will never look back.

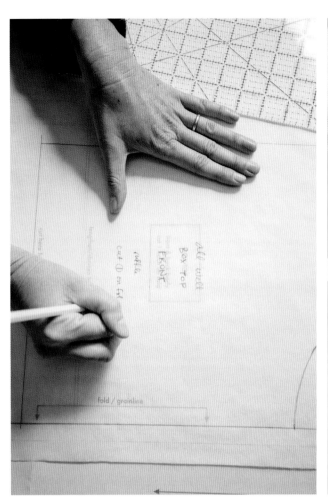

hacking sewing patterns

It might seem obvious, but it's worth saying aloud: The whole point of most sewing patterns is to help you make a specific thing that will turn out a specific way. But there might be more that you want to do beyond just adjusting the pattern: You might want to *hack* the pattern into something new. You can do that! Maybe after sewing a pattern once, the next time you sew it you have the idea to add some poofy sleeves. Or, you want a different kind of collar for your jacket. A lot of the time, if you come up with an idea for a hack, you're sort of on your own,

and you get to figure out how to do it. But the patterns in this book are different: They're designed specifically to be hacked into dozens of unique garments. And you're not on your own: You can mix and match the hacking instructions in this book. Learning how to hack patterns is an amazing way to build your skills in not only sewing but also drafting new designs.

When starting to hack, make yourself a quick copy of the pattern on extra paper by tracing it and cutting it out. That way you won't have to worry about changing or cutting up your original version.

gather fabric and notions

Figure out how much fabric you need: Usually a pattern has a recommended amount of fabric in yards or meters. It can be a bit nuanced: If you're adding length to make a garment longer, you will potentially need more fabric. Keep in mind that fabric shrinks a bit when it's laundered and pressed—for example, about 5% in width and 10% in length for cotton—but it varies widely by the type of fabric. Sometimes this is listed online, or you can ask, or just round up. It just means that you will usually need a bit more fabric than the raw amounts listed on a chart, unless the chart says it accounts for some shrinkage. When you're just beginning, you can be generous with the amount of fabric you get, and then use the scraps for practicing and other projects.

You'll also need notions: thread, at least, and sometimes binding or elastic or buttons or zippers. The pattern will tell you about what you need and how much is recommended—make choices about what you want, make a list, and go gathering. You may also need to check that you have the right needles for the type of fabric you're using, for example silk needles for sewing silk, or heavy-duty needles for very heavy canvas. All-purpose needles will work for most fabrics though.

fabric prepping

For garment sewing, it's good to prewash your fabric before you sew it. Use whatever kind of wash routine you plan to use in the future for your clothes. The idea is to preshrink the fabric so that you don't end up sad that what you made has shrunk beyond repair the first time you wash it, so you might want to wash and dry it on HOT for this first wash, if your fabric can handle that.

The exception is if you're not planning to launder the project in the future—canvas bags or pouches that you will just spot clean over the years, for example—or a very fragile silk garment that you will hand wash in cool water.

We like to wash the fabric right after we buy it, even if we're planning to fold it up and store it a bit before making something. If you're going to store your fabric after washing, give it a quick iron. You will still need to iron it again before you cut it later on, but it helps to get rid of the big creases you get from washing.

Label fabrics if you're not using them right away with little notes to your future self about the fiber content, if it's prewashed and ready to go, and any other useful information. You could use a small piece of paper or masking tape. You can also cut a small swatch out of a corner of the fabric to put in a sewing notebook (see Chapter 20)—that way you can know at a glance what fabrics you have on hand.

test garment/muslin

Making a muslin or test garment is key to deciding whether you like the size you chose based on the pattern's size chart, and whether you want to make any adjustments, or even sew the garment in a different size the next time around. Test garments are like a first draft of your finished garment. Unless you are super confident that a garment will fit you just as you hope on your first sew-through, it's usually worth it to make a test garment, often called a *muslin* or *toile*.

Here's how we like to make test garments:

Choose a test fabric
Find fabric you can use to test. Your fabric store might have inexpensive muslin intended for the purpose, or you could save old sheets (fitted ones can be snipped at the corners to lie flat), or use tablecloths, or fabric from thrift shops or secondhand stores.

Choose a size and cut
Read the size chart and find out what size(s) you fall into for the major points of measurement (like bust, waist, and hip), and find the base size(s) you will be working with. Adjust the pattern for length, arm opening, or other places to make the pattern specific to you, and cut out a copy of the main body pieces from your test fabric. Skip any pockets, collars, or details unless you *really* want to test them. (You can pin on the pattern piece or draw them on with chalk.)

Baste your test garment together
Using a basting stitch—which just means lengthening your regular machine stitch to 5 mm or similar, sew quickly down the main seams. For the box top, that is the shoulder and the side seams. If it's a more complicated garment, you might need to add other pieces, like a waistband, in order to assess the fit. Don't finish the edges or seams.

Try it on
Try the garment on and check the fit in the mirror. If you have a phone that takes video, you could prop it up and take a video of yourself moving around. You can pin or trim the seam allowances at the neckline, arm openings, and/or bottom hem to simulate where they will hit. Try to imagine the difference in drape of your final fabric versus the test fabric and how that will change the fit. Do you like the shape, how it looks? Make markings for adjustments right on the fabric of the test garment.

Assess
Move your body. How does it feel when you move your arms around, cross them in front of you? If you have long sleeves, how is the wrist length feeling? Is the wrist circumference tighter than you like? How is the room in the armpit? Do you want more or less room at the hips? Do you want more ease? Less ease? Try pinning or sewing the fabric to test your ideas out. What does it look like in the mirror now? You might want to wear your muslin around the house for a little while to see how it would feel to live in it.

Make choices and tweaks
After making your muslin, you may decide you'd prefer more or less ease. Remember, the size chart and garment measurements are just a jumping-off point. Change your pattern pieces based on what you learned, what you like, and what you need. Write notes to yourself directly on the pattern.

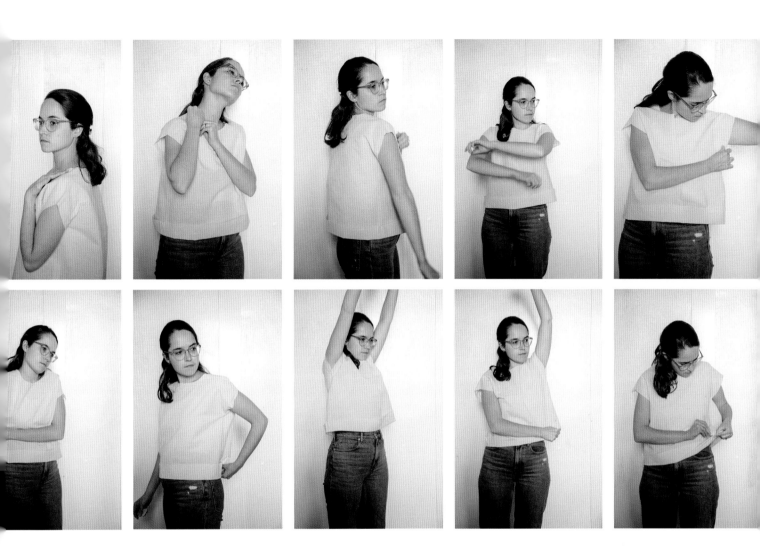

Hang on to it

If you have another version of the same pattern planned, you might want to save your test garment to reuse it. You can fold it up, add a note for your future self, and set it with your fabric and sewing supplies.

Making test garments might sound like a waste of time and fabric, but it's something we really wish we'd been encouraged to do earlier as we were learning to sew. It's especially valuable when there are a lot of fit variables, as with pants or things meant to be worn close to the body. Just because you're sewing a garment with the pattern supposedly in your "size" doesn't mean it will fit your unique body the way you want it to without any tweaks. (This is similar to trying on clothes at a store.) It would feel even more wasteful to have sewn up a garment in your good fabric that you don't end up wearing because the fit is off. That's a bad feeling! We've been there.

reading sewing instructions

It's always good to fully read through the instructions before cutting and sewing. So many times we've caught some useful information that we might have missed. It also really helps to have a big-picture view of what's ahead.

Think about using a recipe to cook dinner or bake a cake—you always want to read through the instructions before you start to see what's coming up. Maybe you need to preheat the oven. Maybe you need to set the butter out to soften. Maybe you're missing a crucial ingredient. When you read the pattern instructions in full, you get to mentally rehearse the steps, see if there are any things you've never tried before or that you're unsure about. You can do a little more research, ask a friend, and practice that bit on scraps when you come to it. And then, knowing what lies ahead, you dive in!

ironing your fabric before you cut

Right before you are going to cut the pieces out, give your fabric a nice thorough iron, pressing it all over so it's smooth. You're mostly aiming to get out any stubborn wrinkles from washing or storing to make it easier to cut accurately. This sets you up for accurate sewing and a beautiful finished

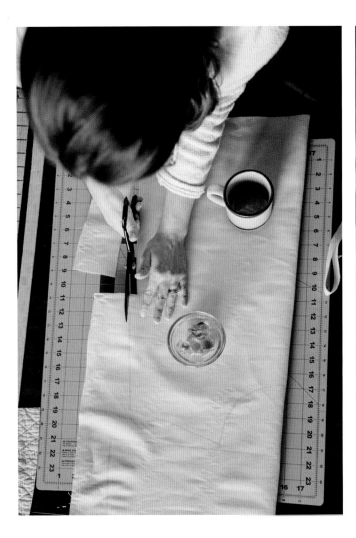

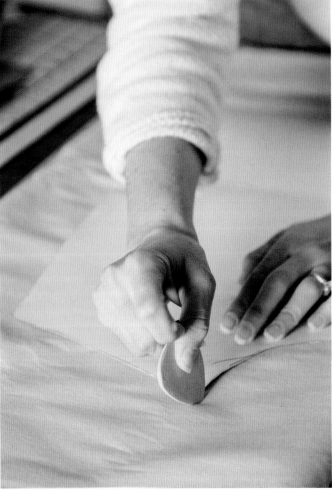

project with fewer fitting problems. Steam ironing also helps some fabrics shrink a tiny bit to a more stable state.

finding the grain and laying out the fabric

The straight grain will be more obvious in some fabrics than others. Lay the fabric out on the floor or table where you plan to cut, and tug it, adjust, and gently use your fingertips to scoot it around so the selvage edge is straight and the rest of the fabric is neatly aligned with it. If the fabric has been stored for a long time on a roll, you might really have to do some work to get it in shape. One way to find the cross grain is by cutting into the fabric perpendicular to the selvage, then ripping across, then stretching it back into place before folding or cutting. It can be helpful to watch videos or look at blogs. It's a hard thing to describe in words.

reading pattern markings

Take a good look at the pattern pieces. You will probably see that they have the name of the pattern, the name of the piece (like "front body" or "sleeve" or "pocket") and how many copies of that piece to cut out. They also have markings that you will quickly learn how to read:

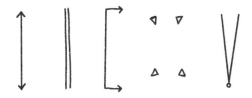

- *Grain markings*: usually a long double-headed arrow; these help you line your pattern pieces up with the fabric's straight grain.
- *Lengthen/shorten lines*: places where the designer recommends you cut the pattern and either overlap (to subtract length) or tape in new paper if you want to add length.
- *Cut on fold*: the pattern piece will tell you whether to cut flat or on folded fabric and will show you where the fold should go. Fold marks can often also serve as grain arrows; the fold almost always follows the grain for clothes patterns.

- *Notches*: match points or reference points to help you as you sew, so you can match a notch on one piece to a notch on another. To transfer them to your fabric, either cut the notch triangles outward from the seam allowance or use snips to make a very short cut into the seam allowance to mark the notches.
- *Darts*: typically used for bust or hip/waist shaping.

When you run into pattern markings that you're not familiar with, look through the pattern's instruction booklet or, if that fails, try looking online or in books to find out more.

arranging pattern pieces on the fabric

Lay out your pattern pieces on your ironed, smoothed-out, grain-aligned fabric. Carefully line up the pattern pieces' grainline arrows ↕, with the fabric's straight grain. Typically pieces are laid out parallel to the selvage of the fabric, unless the pattern piece says it is intended to be cut on the bias ↘ or cross grain ↔. Keep all the pattern pieces consistent as you lay them out: Don't do some parallel to the grain and some at right angles to it. All the arrows on the different pattern pieces should point in the same direction, like this ↕ ↕ ↕ (not like this ↕ ↔ although sometimes it doesn't matter quite as much for bags).

When pieces are marked for you to cut them on the fold, place the fold mark on the pattern on the fold of the fabric. Make a clean fold with no bubbles in either layer of fabric, keeping the grain consistent on both layers. It's common to get off grain and not realize it when you move the top layer and it gets out of alignment with the (hidden) bottom layer. Just take a bit of care with this step.

- -

TIP! A pattern piece that is marked to be cut on the fold can be cut flat instead if you'd prefer. You can trace the folded pattern piece onto another sheet of paper and tape them together where the fold would be so you have the full shape ready to trace onto just one layer of fabric, or just flip the piece to add a mirror image to the other side after tracing. Handy for shifty fabrics or pattern Tetris.

- -

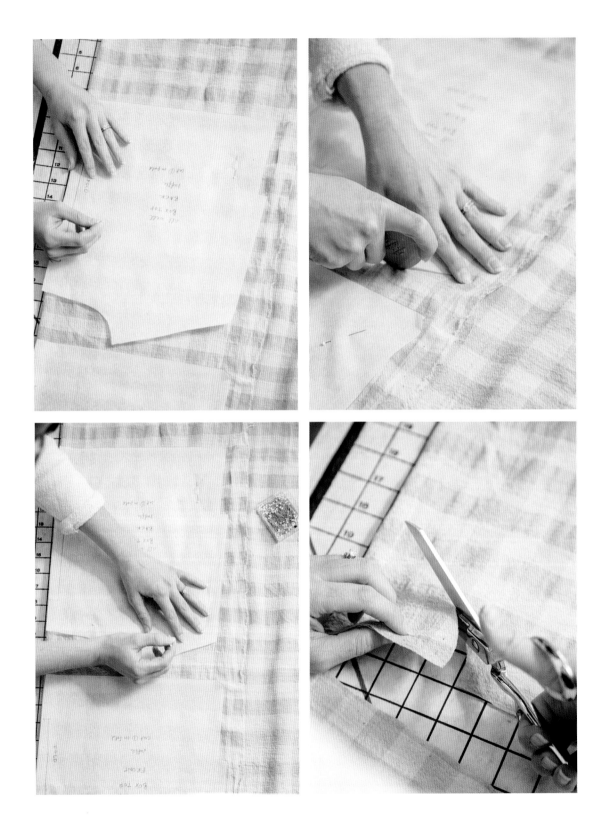

ALL WELL - - - - - - - How to Sew Clothes

Another thing to keep an eye out for is cutting two copies of the same pattern piece—many times you will need to cut mirror images, so that you have one right side and one left side. The angled pockets on the cardigan coat in this book are a good example. Mirroring happens automatically if you're cutting two layers at once on folded fabric, but if you're cutting the pieces out flat, one at a time, flip the pattern piece over before cutting the second one. This might not matter so much if your fabric is the same on both sides, but it really matters if your fabric has a visibly different right side and wrong side.

Some patterns will have suggested pattern layouts for how to fit the needed pattern pieces in the amount of fabric they recommend, but there are always lots of different ways to put the puzzle together. As long as you're keeping a close eye on the fabric grain and grain guidelines on the pattern pieces and making sure you're cutting on the fold when needed, you can fit everything together however you want.

When you've finalized your placements, pin the pattern pieces in place, or weigh them down with pattern weights or other things you have on hand, like books.

If you're using scissors, trace the pattern pieces with some sort of marking tool like chalk; then gently remove the pattern before cutting. You can also use a rotary cutter, ruler, and cutting mat—either mark with chalk or other marking tools or carefully cut directly around the pattern pieces. This is also the time to transfer important pattern markings like notches onto your fabric. Once all the pattern pieces are laid out, you're ready to cut.

taking a deep breath

This is a big moment! You're about to cut your fabric! You might be thinking, *What if I mess up, waste my fabric or my time?* Big feelings! Take a breath. Take a sip of water or tea. The only way through is to start. If something goes wrong, you can always try again. Take a second look at your pattern pieces and your fabric, and go for it! Cut away!

- - - - - - - - - - - - - - - - - - - -

ABOUT THE INSTRUCTIONS
IN THIS BOOK

This book's instructions are intentionally long and detailed, compared to most sewing patterns. What can we say? We're writers, we're naturally verbose! But, beyond that, it's really important to us that people making their very first box tops, or cardigan coats, or bags will feel welcome and comfortable, so we try to avoid jargon and shortcuts and pay extra attention to clarity and completeness. If you're an advanced sewist, you may find you don't need these extra tips or descriptions. That's great! You probably already know how to sew a box top, or insert a zipper successfully, so feel free to skim mostly for the details and seam allowances and particularities of each garment or bag and use the diagrams as your guide.

- -

ABOUT THE DIAGRAMS IN THIS BOOK

In sewing pattern instruction diagrams, typically one side is shaded and the other is light to differentiate between right and wrong sides of the fabric. In this book the *wrong side* is shaded. We like to think of it as how the inside of a garment is shadowy and the outside is lighter, if you hold it up.

For visual simplicity, we left some of the more subtle shape details out of our instruction diagrams. Also, your garments and pattern pieces will look a little different from the diagrams, since the proportions vary depending on what size you're sewing and how tall you are.

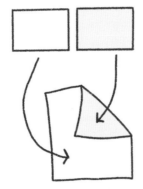

sew sew sew!

Now it's time to sew! In some ways, this is the least tiring or confusing part. Most of the big decisions are already made, and what is left is a string of small tasks, one at a time. Keep a close eye on the instructions as you sew—try not to work too far ahead without checking back in. If you run into anything you're confused about as you're following the instructions, you might want to try practicing that skill on a scrap of fabric or doing some searching to find a more detailed explanation. If you've messed things up, try to fix the mistake as soon as you notice it. Seam-rip now, or press more accurately now, or sort out why the inseams don't match now, instead of carrying on and letting the mistake grow. You are free to start and stop whenever you want, take breaks, listen to music, and see how things are shaping up along the way. You can try on what you're sewing, and make adjustments as you go if you want.

what sounds fun?

We've spent quite a few pages gearing up to make things in this book, and now we're switching over to *sewing clothes* and *sewing bags*. Exciting! As you read through, think about what you want to sew first. What seems like something that could help you to build your skills and learn by doing? What are you excited to wear or use? What order of projects might make sense? We've ordered things in a particular progression of skills, but feel free to ignore our chronology and follow the fun. We're in *your* studio now! What do you want to make?

PART II

THE BOX TOPS

– – – – – – – – – – – – – – –

The Box Top,
Box Dress,
and Variations

Chapter 7

The Box Top

AMY: This pattern was in development for a long, long time. First, it was a self-drafted personal garment—I traced the pattern onto a piece of poster board I bought at Target so I could use it again and again. I made a few versions early in my garment-sewing days and wore them to threadbareness. I still wear many of those early box tops today! The box top became the basis for an earlier iteration of All Well, a super-small made-to-order clothing line, where I tweaked the pattern and expanded it into multiple sizes and variations, and really fine-tuned the sewing process by production-sewing it over 100 times.

Now it is a bestselling sewing pattern, tweaked and perfected even more, something you can make yourself, customize to your body and your style, and wear until it's threadbare. That was the dream all along, really. The more I came to love this pattern, the more I came to want to share it with anyone who wanted to make it. There are a lot of similar boxy top patterns out there, but I really do think this one is special. It's a true building block, a pattern to learn and grow with. A really great first sewing project or hundredth sewing project.

If you're looking for a place to start, this is a good one. The box top is really a sort of blank canvas for beautiful fabric to shine. Box tops are generally meant to be worn *boxy*, aka with a good bit of ease. This is designed to be a loose garment, to hang pleasingly away from the body. For the most basic box top, you will just need two pattern pieces.

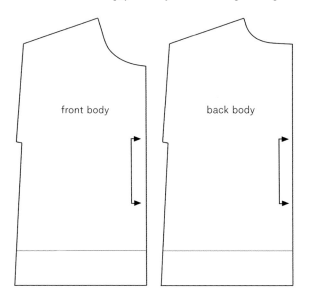

front body   back body

Even if you're going to make the other variations, read through the box top instructions in this chapter first for detailed advice on choosing fabric, sizing and pattern adjustments, and so on.

how to choose a size

Use your body measurements and the finished garment measurement chart to choose the size you want to sew. Keep in mind that our size numbers don't correspond to typical US or international dress sizes that you may be used to. That's by design. We recommend that you choose a size that is 6"–8" (15 cm–20 cm) larger than the measurement around your bust/chest. We've included our size recommendations based on your body measurement in the bust column—look for your measurement there for the quickest way to pick a size.

Box Top Size Chart

Size Number	Size Letter	Bust Finished Garment Circumference		Bust (for recommended ease)	
		inches	cm	inches	cm
1	S	40	102	32–34	81–86
2	M	44	112	36–38	91–97
3	L	48	122	40–42	102–107
4	XL	54	138	44–48	112–122
5	2XL	60	152.5	50–56	127–142
6	3XL	66	168	56–62	142–157

If your bust measurement means you fall between sizes, you can choose to go up or down a size, depending on whether you'd prefer a more snug or looser fit. The more ease you choose, the more roominess you will have in your box top.

You might like to play around with which size you choose for your box top. Try to make one with more ease, try one with less ease, see what feels best. How the finished garment looks on the body also varies a lot with fabric choice.

choosing fabrics

The box top pattern is designed specifically to work for woven fabrics in a range of different weights and drapes. Starting with a mid-weight woven fabric that isn't too slippery—like one about 5 oz/yd^2 or about 170 gsm in linen, raw silk, or cotton—is probably a good bet for seeing how this pattern works on your body. Do you prefer drapey, flowy lightweight fabric? Try a lightweight silk or cotton lawn. Are you into super structural-looking garments? Try canvas or denim—though anything above 9 oz/yd^2 (305 gsm) is probably verging on too stiff. You could even sew this pattern in a knit fabric that has very little (like almost zero) stretch.

We've made box tops in all sorts of different fabrics, and we love seeing how the fit changes with different drapes. Different fabrics drape differently, and therefore they react to ease differently too—you might try going up or down one size number in different fabrics. A light fabric will typically drape dramatically, almost bringing in the ease on its own, to lie closer to the body with lots of movement. A heavier and less drapey fabric will stay stiffer and keep its shape, emphasizing the amount of ease, appearing more boxy.

what you need

The following charts show the recommended amount of fabric for each variation. The amounts are generous to allow for shrinkage from prewashing—you might be able to use less.

For sizes 1–3, the standard 60" (150 cm) width fabric lets you fit both body pieces on a double fold, so you can fit a sleeveless box top onto 1 yard (0.75 meter). To do this, fold the fabric in from each side, so the two selvege edges meet in the middle. Then place the front body on one of the folds, and the back body on the other fold before cutting them out.

Box Top Fabric Requirements, Sizes 1–3

SIZES 1–3	45" wide (yds)	115 cm wide (m)	60" wide (yds)	150 cm wide (m)
Sleeveless Box Top	1.5	1.5	1	0.75
Long Sleeve Box Top	2.25	2.25	1.5	1.5
Sleeveless Ruffle Top (Sizes 1-2)	2.25	2.25	2.25	2.25
Sleeveless Ruffle Top (Size 3)	3.25	3	2.25	2.25
Sleeveless Box Dress	2.75	2.75	1.5	1.5

Box Top Fabric Requirements, Sizes 4–6

For sizes 4–6, the fabric lengths indicated are the same for the different widths of fabric available on the market.

SIZES 4–6	45" wide or 60" wide (yds)	115 cm or 150 cm wide (m)
Sleeveless Box Top	2	1.75
Long Sleeve Box Top	2.5	2.5
Sleeveless Ruffle Top (Sizes 4-6)	4	3.5
Sleeveless Box Dress	3.5	3.25

In addition to the body pieces, cut a neck binding piece on the bias: A 1" wide by 32" long (2.5 cm by 81 cm) strip of fabric. This can be the same fabric as the rest of the top or another fabric you have on hand. See Chapter 19 (page 170) for instructions on how to make a bias binding strip. Or you can buy some 1/4" (6 mm) double-fold bias tape, which is 1" (2.5 cm) wide when unfolded.

pattern adjustments

You can adjust the length, the arm opening at the biceps, and the scoop and width of the neckline. You can also grade between sizes (page 62) so you use different sizes at different places (for example, at the bust and hips). We love how the boxy shape looks on all bodies so we intentionally excluded darts from this pattern, but you may prefer to add some bust darts to offset some of the ease at the bust and waist. We recommend making a muslin and choosing and testing out your fit adjustments before proceeding to your main fabric. Here are some places where you might want to adjust the pattern:

- *Arm Opening*: Lengthen or shorten the arm openings as much as desired by adding or subtracting length from the *bottom* of the arm opening. Redraw the horizontal line at the bottom of the arm opening back toward the side seamline at the desired spot.
- *Neckline*: You can scoop, unscoop, widen, or narrow the neckline as desired. If you widen or narrow it, redraw the shoulder seamlines to blend toward the new neck opening point. Be careful not to change the neck so much that the shoulder angles become dramatically different than they were to start—this could affect the way the top hangs on your shoulders.
- *Length Adjustment*: The pattern was drafted for a person who is 5'3" (160 cm) tall. If you are much taller or shorter than this, you may want to adjust the length of the pattern pieces before you cut your fabric. If you're planning on a box top that goes down to and past your hip, check for the ease there too—you will want at least 6" (15 cm) of ease at the hip. To lengthen the pattern, cut at the *lengthen/shorten* marks on the pattern piece, and either spread apart and tape in more paper to add length or overlap pieces to remove length.

Then use a ruler to draw a new, smooth seamline and edge. Make the same adjustment to the back body.

fit guidelines

The box top has a lot of flexibility for fit, but here are some things you might want to think about:

LENGTH: This is very subjective. You may be going for a crop top, around belly-button level, or for the regular length, for which it should hit near the top of the hips.

HEAD HOLE/WIDTH OF OPENING ACROSS NECK: The opening should dip just below your collarbones. Feel free to adjust the neckline as desired.

ARM OPENING: The goal is for the top to not be too constricting on your biceps/arms, but not so low under the arms that it reveals anything you don't want to show. (This can depend a lot on the fabric and how you want to style it.)

Now it's time to sew! *If you are using these instructions to sew a test garment, sew only the shoulder and side seams, skip the seam finishing and binding of the neckline and arm openings, and pin up the seam allowance at the hem. Then try the test garment on to check the fit.*

sewing instructions

cut your fabric

1. For the box top, you will just need a front body and a back body piece, each cut on the fold, plus a strip of neckline binding. Now you're ready to sew!

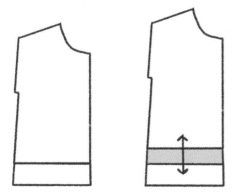

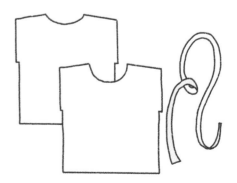

shoulder and side seams

2. Align the front body and back body, right sides together, and pin along the top shoulder seams. Sew the shoulder seams with a 1/2" (13 mm) seam allowance.

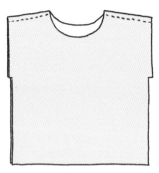

3. Press seams open to help them settle into themselves, then press them back together so you can finish the raw edges of the seam allowances as desired. Finish them, then press seams toward the back of the garment.
4. Align the front body and back body, right sides together, and pin along side seams.
5. Sew the side seams with a 1/2" (13 mm) seam allowance, starting at the underarms. Sew a gentle curve to navigate the corner, then continue sewing down the main side seams.

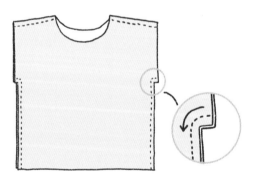

6. Finish side seams as desired, and press toward the back of the garment.

finish arm opening

7. Snip a small cut into the seam allowance of the underarm curve to aid your armhole hemming. Aim your snip for the center of the underarm curve, as indicated in the diagram. Be very careful to not cut through your stitches; only cut the seam allowance. (It's fine to cut through the finishing stitches though.) Press the side seams' seam allowances toward the back of the garment.

8. Press the arm opening seam allowances' raw edges toward the wrong side of the fabric 1/4" (6 mm) and then another 1/4" (6 mm) to make what's called a double-fold hem. It may help to pin your work.
9. Edgestitch all the way around the folded edge, starting on the back of the garment near the bottom of the arm opening and working your way around. Take care to cover the raw edges from where you snipped the seam allowance in your double-fold hem, and tuck it into the hem to secure it.

10. Repeat steps 7-9 to finish the other arm opening.

neckline binding

11. Time to bind your neckline. Grab your strip of binding
fabric and turn to Chapter 19 on page 170 for instructions
for how to sew the neckline. This is a technique
you'll probably find yourself using on lots of different
garments, not just box tops.

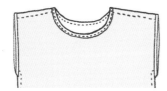

hem

12. Press the bottom edge of the garment up 1/4" (6 mm)
toward the wrong side, then fold up 1/4" (6 mm) *again*
to form your hem. Make sure to keep the side seam
allowances pressed toward the back of the garment.
Pin in place.

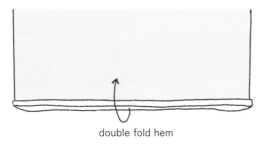

double fold hem

13. Edgestitch along the edge of the fold all the way
around the hem.

finished

14. You did it! A beautiful box top! Give it a wash and
wear it everywhere.

Chapter 8

Long Sleeve
Box Top

The long sleeve box top is a staple piece for layering and really shines when the weather is cool. If you have a box top you like, try it on and see how it feels as you mull your ideal long sleeve version. You might decide you want to size up for a slightly more oversized look—this works especially well on the long sleeve version. Also, think about what you will wear under or over it, and how bulky the fabric you're using is. (Will it fit under a cardigan?) There are a lot of design choices you can make to get very different results each time you sew this pattern.

Refer to Chapter 7 for the size chart, fabric needs, and tips for sewing and fitting the box top in general. For the long sleeve box top, these are the pattern pieces you will need:

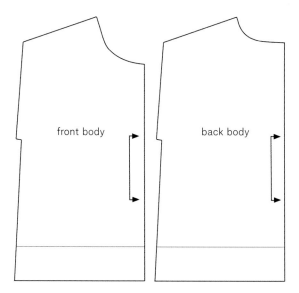

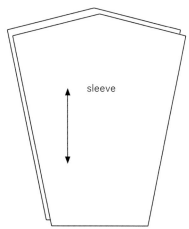

Look at the shape of the sleeve pattern piece: this is a really simple sleeve. Without swoopy curves or a lot of shaping, it gives you a nice boxy fit and look. It's fairly simple to sew, a great first try at sleeves, and just a little more complicated than the regular box top construction-wise. Before, you were working with just two very similar front and back pieces; now you're adding a new step where you sew the sleeve on. And it's a place to experiment with making simple adjustments to pattern pieces to change the length or width of the sleeve. If you're just getting started with sewing clothes, this is a good building block for skills you can use later, when you'll probably try set-in sleeves that are curved and just a little trickier.

pattern adjustments

You can make all the same adjustments as you made for the box top (see page 79), plus a few more now that you have sleeves. As you sew a test garment, look for room in the armpits, the right length in the sleeves, and cross your arms and hug yourself and otherwise move around to make sure you have enough space in the shoulders. Do you want to wear the sleeves cuffed? Add a little extra length. Or consider adjusting the arm openings at the shoulders or wrists for a little more or less space. Once you've chosen and tested your adjustments, you're ready to sew.

- *Wrist Opening Adjustment*: The sleeve has a close-fitting wrist opening, which you might want to adjust to your own measurements or preferences for ease. (For example, do you like pushing your sleeves partway up your arm?) Add or subtract the desired amount on each side of the pattern piece's wrist opening line. Then, starting all the way up at the outer edges of the shoulder, use a ruler to redraw the two side seam angles of the arm to the new outer edges of the wrist.

- *Sleeve Length Adjustment*: Cut at the *lengthen/shorten* marks on the pattern piece, and either spread the parts apart and tape in more paper (to add length) or overlap the parts (to remove length). Then use a ruler to connect the outer edges of the wrist and the outer edges of the shoulder by drawing a new, smooth edge. Fold the sleeve pattern in half lengthwise and double-check that your adjusted edges are symmetrical, and even them up if necessary.

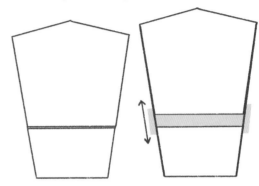

- *Arm Opening Adjustment*: See this adjustment in the box top instructions on page 79—the front body, back body, and sleeve pieces get sewn together, so if you made an adjustment to the front and back, add or subtract the same amount to the top of the sleeve as you did to the body pieces. Then draw a new side edge all the way down to the wrist on the sleeve pattern.

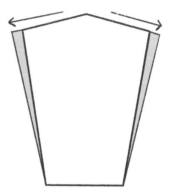

sewing instructions

cut your fabric

1. First, you will need to cut your fabric. Cut your front body and back body pieces on the fold; then cut two sleeves and a bias strip. (See page 176 for making bias strips.)

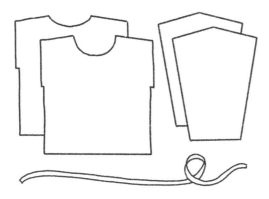

shoulder seams

2. Sew the front body and back body together at the shoulder seams, as instructed in steps 2 and 3 of the box top on page 80.

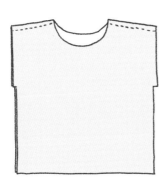

- -

TIP! We <u>don't recommend</u> French seams in this view. Unless you have a very fine fabric, like thin silk, you will end up with too much bulk and unwieldiness around the curve of the arm and at the armpit.

- -

sew sleeves

3. Separate the two body pieces so they're stretched open, with the shoulder seams pressed toward the back of the garment. Pin one sleeve to the joined front and back body, right sides together. Match the middle point of the sleeve to the shoulder seam of the front and back body.

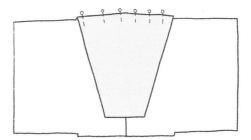

4. Sew the sleeve to the front and back body with 1/2" (13 mm) seam allowance. You will notice that the top of the sleeve is more like a triangle, while the arm opening is more like a straight line. Gently guide the triangle of the sleeve to fit with the shape of the arm opening, while maintaining a 1/2" (13 mm) seam allowance. Ensure that the top shoulder seam allowances remain pressed toward the back body as you sew over them.

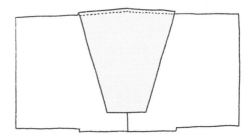

5. Repeat steps 3 and 4 to attach the other sleeve.
6. Finish sleeve seams as desired. Press the sleeve seam allowances out toward the sleeves, away from the bodice (front and back body).

side seams

7. Fold the garment so right sides are together, and the sleeves and front and back body pieces are aligned. Now it's starting to look like a shirt! Pin the sleeve closed and pin the side seams of the front and back body together (making sure to match up the seam lines at the armpit).

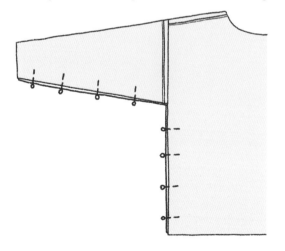

8. Sew a 1/2" (13 mm) seam all the way from wrist to hem. In the underarm area, sew a gentle *curve* rather than pivoting at the angle where the two pieces join. A curve will be much easier to press neatly than an angle. As you sew, make sure the seam allowance where the sleeve was joined to the body is pointing outward toward the sleeve rather than inward toward the front and back body.

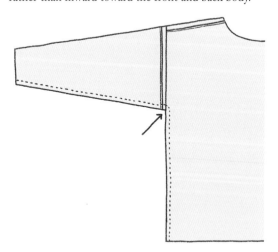

9. Repeat steps 7 and 8 for the other sleeve and side.
10. Finish side seams as desired (serger or zigzag recommended).
11. Press side seams toward the back of the garment.
12. For both sleeves, press the raw edge at the wrist in 1/4" (6 mm) toward the wrong side, then turn over another 1/2" (13 mm) fold to prepare the hem.
13. Edgestitch along the hem to finish the wrist openings.

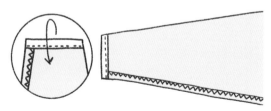

neckline binding and hem

14. To bind the neckline, see instructions in Chapter 19 on page 170.
15. To finish the bottom raw edge, press the bottom edge of the garment up 1/4" (6 mm) toward the wrong side, then 1/4" (6 mm) again to form your hem. Make sure to keep the side seam allowances pressed toward the back of the garment. Pin in place.

finished

16. Flip your garment right side out, give it a final press. Hooray, a long sleeve box top!

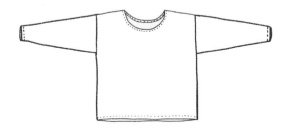

Chapter 9

Ruffle Box Top or
Ruffle Dress

It's the box top, but flouncy and fancy! Ruffles aren't necessarily for every day or everyone, but when the mood arises they're so much fun. The box top is the perfect pattern to add some ruffles to—its simplicity shows off the drape of the fabric and keeps the extra drama of a ruffle from becoming too much. Make it a dress for a classic silhouette with a twirly skirt, or a top for even more versatility and layering possibilities. Feel free to add sleeves for a long sleeve ruffle top or dress.

The ruffle dress is basically just a cropped box top, with a rectangular ruffle piece attached below.

fabric thoughts

The ruffle means that the structure and weight of the fabric have even more importance than usual for how it will feel to wear. There's so much fabric! Does it stand off your body and keep you cool? Does it flow with you and hug your shape? What feeling do you want? Keep these questions in mind when you're choosing fabric. This style will work best on light- to medium-weight fabrics with more drape and flow to them. Heavier fabrics are harder to gather.

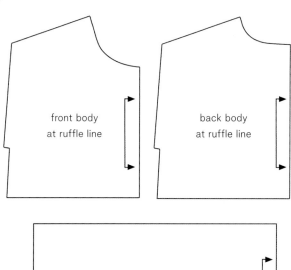

pattern adjustments

You can make all the same adjustments as you would to the box top (page 77) or the long sleeve box top (page 82). You can adjust the ruffle to make more or fewer gathers, and in the next section we will explain how to lengthen the ruffle to make a ruffle dress.

- *Adjust gathers*: If you want more or fewer gathers (if you'd like to use less fabric, for example, or if you want *more drama*), you can simply adjust the width of the ruffle pattern pieces as desired. The wider the ruffle pattern, the more gathers; the narrower, the fewer. As long as the width of each ruffle piece (when not folded) is wider than the bottom edge of the box top body, you will have *some* gathering. Feel free to play with the width of the ruffle pieces to suit the amount of fabric you have, or your personal style preferences.
- *Adjust top length:* Want the bodice to hit a little lower down, or higher up? Use a ruler to redraw the body hemline.

add length to make a ruffle dress

Simple gathered dresses are timeless, and so easy to wear. All you have to do is lengthen the ruffle pieces, then sew following the instructions. The easy way to do this is to just cut the ruffle pieces *longer*, taking a guess at how much longer—you could always cut it shorter if you overshoot. If you want to be precise about it, here's a more official way:

1. Grab a measuring tape and hold it in the center of your body at the spot between your collarbones. Decide exactly how long you'd like your dress to be. Maybe a little above the knee, maybe a little below the knee, maybe ankle length. It's totally up to you! Look in a mirror or ask a friend to help you see the measuring tape reading at the length you like. Make sure you stand straight and tall when you get the reading. A good trick is to mark your desired length on the clothes you're wearing by pinning a large safety pin horizontally and then threading your measuring tape through it—that keeps your measuring tape steady and gives you a good visual reference point to read the tape at the right spot. Write down your *desired length measurement*.

2. Next, figure out the *existing finished* ruffle-top *length*. Measure the front body pattern piece and ruffle pattern pieces in your size, and calculate:

(length of the front body ____ + length of ruffle ___) – 1 3/4" (4.5 cm) = [existing length]

NOTE: Take your bodice measurement along the center fold line of the front body piece, from the base of the neck curve down to the crop line.

3. Now figure out *how much length to add* to the existing ruffle pattern piece to get the dress to the length you'd like:

(desired length from step 1 ____) – (existing ruffle-top length from step 2 ____) = (length of ruffle to add)

4. Add the length you calculated in step 3 to your ruffle pattern piece along the shorter edge of the rectangle. When you go to cut the ruffle pieces, use a ruler to add that desired amount of length and cut.

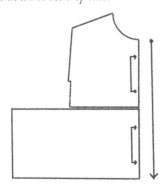

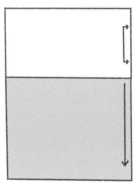

sewing instructions

cut your fabric

1. First, cut your fabric. You will need a front body and back body piece, cut to the crop line (or wherever you'd like the division from bodice to ruffle to be), a bias strip for neckline binding, and two ruffle pieces, either shirt length or dress length. It will look like this for the ruffle top:

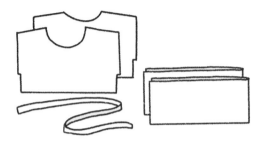

And like this for the ruffle dress (or maybe your ruffle piece will be even longer!):

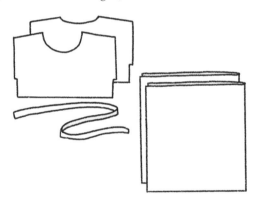

sew the top like a regular box top

2. The bodice of the ruffle top is just a dramatically cropped box top. Follow steps 2-11 of the sewing instructions for the box top, beginning on page 80. When you get to the part about the bottom hem, stop—it's ruffle time! Come back here and continue on. We'll call the assembled front and back part *the bodice* in the rest of the instructions. You're leaving the bottom edge of the bodice raw because this is where you will attach the ruffle. It should look like this:

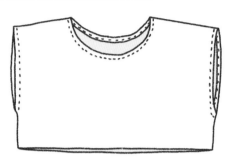

sew ruffle

3. Align the two ruffle pieces with right sides together. Sew them together on one short side with a 1/2" (13 mm) seam allowance to connect the two pieces into one very long strip. Finish the seam as desired. (*The diagrams show a ruffle top; the ruffle dress has the same instructions, but your ruffle piece will just look longer.*)

4. Increase your stitch length to a long basting stitch, around 5 mm. Pull your sewing machine thread tails (on both bobbin and top thread) out a little longer than you would for a normal seam, and make sure they are both in place and untangled before beginning to sew.

5. You are going to make two lines of basting stitches across the width of the ruffle. Do not backstitch at the beginning or end. Make sure you have at least an inch or two (2.5–5 cm) of extra thread for both the top and bobbin threads hanging off each end.

a. Sew one line of basting stitches along the top (one long side) of the ruffle strip, 1/4" (6 mm) from the raw edge of the fabric. At the end of the line of basting stitches, pull your sewing machine threads out a little longer than usual, about 7" (18 cm), and snip.

b. Repeat to sew another line of basting stitches 3/8" (1 cm) from the raw edge of the fabric. You will now have two parallel lines of basting stitches and four threads hanging loose from each side of the long ruffle strip.

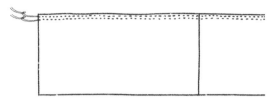

6. On one end of the ruffle, separate the front two threads from the back two threads of the basting stitching lines. Insert a pin into the fabric near the end of the ruffle (see diagram for placement)—you will use it as an anchor point. Wrap the front two threads around the pin until secure.

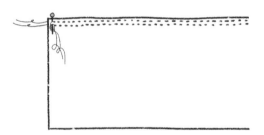

7. Slowly and carefully pull on the back two threads to gather the fabric and create the ruffles. Use your fingers to evenly distribute the fabric gathers. Start by gathering only one half of the ruffle, up until the center seam.

8. You're done gathering this half when the width matches your bodice front width, plus 1/2" (13 mm) for the seam allowance you will use later to sew the ruffle together into a circle. Lay the ruffle next to the bodice to check.

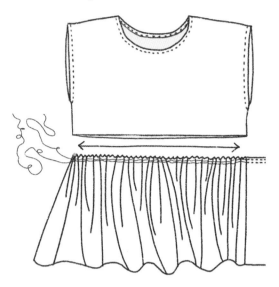

9. Wrap the back two threads of the gathered side of the ruffle around the anchor pin to "lock" the ruffle and make sure it doesn't undo itself while you work with the other side.

10. Repeat the gathering process with the other side of the ruffle until its width matches the width of the first side of the ruffle. Fold in half to check, or use a ruler. When the width matches, wrap the back threads around the anchor pin to "lock" the gathers in place and to make sure they don't unravel.

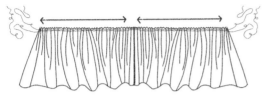

- -

TIP! Frustrated with this gathering method? Some people prefer the zigzag and string method. Instead of the two rows of parallel basting stitches, you can use the zigzag stitch on your sewing machine. Sew a zigzag (the widest your machine has) along the top edge of your ruffle piece within the seam allowance, carefully laying a thin piece of string (or dental floss) underneath your zigzag stitch as you sew, right in the middle. Your string will be surrounded by the stitches like it's in a tunnel—be careful not to snag it. Then you can gather the fabric by pushing it along the string. If you need to see an example of this method, try a quick online search. It might make gathering more enjoyable for you.

- -

attach ruffle

11. With right sides of bodice and ruffle together, pin the gathered edge of the ruffle to the raw bottom edge of the bodice all the way around. Make sure to align the ruffle's center seam and one of the side seams of the bodice—it doesn't matter which one.

12. Change your stitch length back to your normal setting (probably around 2.5 mm). With the ruffle pinned on top of the bodice, sew the ruffle to the bodice using a 1/2" (13 mm) seam allowance. We recommend you start at the matched bodice side seam and ruffle center seam and attach one complete side of the ruffle before going back and attaching the other. Make sure to leave unsewn the final 1/2" (13 mm) on each end of the ruffle (which should extend beyond the width of the bodice). This will be the seam allowance for the second side seam.

- -

TIP! Watch that your gathers aren't shifting as you sew the ruffle to the bodice, leaving areas that are more flat and areas that are more gathered. Aim to distribute the gathers as evenly as you can initially, and then redistribute while you sew as needed. Pinning to keep them in place could be helpful here.

- -

13. Once the ruffle is attached to the bodice, sew the second ruffle side seam as follows:

    a. With right sides together, sew a 1/2" (13 mm) seam to join the ruffle side seam to make a continuous circle, making sure not to catch the bodice fabric at the top of the seam.

    b. Finish the seam as desired.

    c. Tack the second ruffle side seam allowance toward the front of the garment by aligning it with the bodice side seam (which should be pressed toward the back of the garment) and making about an inch (2.5 cm) of stitches over the ruffle seam allowance above the existing side seam to tack it in place.

14. Finish the ruffle seam (along the circumference of the garment, where it attaches to the bodice) as desired. (We find sergers most helpful here, but you could also do some zigzag.)

15. Press the ruffle seam allowance up toward the top of the garment. Press or steam this seam well to ensure the ruffle lies flat.

hem

16. Turn your garment right side out.

17. Press the seam where the ruffle connects to the bodice again, this time from the right side of the garment. This gives it extra crispness—make sure it lies correctly. (The seam allowance inside points up toward the shoulders.)

18. *Optional*: If your fabric is *really* having a hard time lying flat, you can sew a line of topstitching around the bodice, through the ruffle/bodice seam allowance, holding it up toward the top of the garment. This isn't necessary for most fabrics.

19. Press the bottom raw edge of the ruffle up toward the wrong side 1/4" (6 mm), then 1/4" (6 mm) again to make a double-fold hem. Edgestitch near the edge of the double fold all the way around the bottom ruffle edge to hem your garment.

finished

20. You made a ruffle top! Hooray!

Or maybe a ruffle dress! Double hooray!

Chapter 10

Box Top Variations

After you've sewn the patterns as they're written (or even the first time you're sewing them), there are so many features and hacks you can add to your box tops to make them your own. For each technique, we'll cover what it is, suggest when you might use it for greatest effect, and give instructions and drawings to show you how to do it. You can then jump over here at any point in sewing the main variations in the instructions to customize. Plus, these hacks will work on many other garments you sew too—the skills are transferable.

Dress, belt, split hem, high-low hem, patch pockets, extra-deep hem, French seams: There are lots of ideas here for how to wear and style, and you can mix and match them in combination too. What if you made the dress hack, but with long sleeves, and a split hem? Or the simple box top, but with cute patch pockets and French seams? This is the point where we often let the fabric help make the choices: often as you feel it and see it, you'll start to envision just the right details for the garment it's destined to become.

One thing to know about hacks in this book: In most cases, we chose the simplest method for adding each element—we leaned toward accessibility rather than ultra-professional finishes. There are lots of ways to add a collar or attach a sleeve, lots of ways to sew buttonholes, some more complicated than others, and there are lots of ideas from lots of people about the best way to do everything. Treat the hacking instructions as a jumping-off point, and do things differently, consult the internet, call your friends or relatives, and ask for advice as much as you want. That's what we do too!

french seams

French seams go great with the box top, box dress, and ruffle top or dress. (We don't recommend them on the long sleeve box top though.) They take a little longer to sew, but make your clothes feel really fancy, and the sturdiness of the seams helps them last a long time. French seams are really good for delicate fabrics like silk, or thin fabrics prone to fraying, like some linens. See the instructions in Chapter 19 (page 176).

split hem

A split hem is a great elevating detail for your box top. Not only does it give you a little extra room in the hips (always comfy), it also looks cool!

The split hem will work great on any of the box tops or the box dress, except for the ruffle top. It's an especially great variation for the box dress—very stylish, and there is more room for your legs as you go confidently striding about town! A split hem or side vent length of 3"–6" (7.5–15 cm) is a good amount for a box dress. See how to sew a split hem in Chapter 19 (page 178).

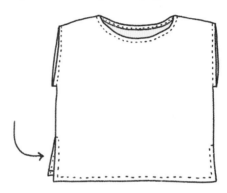

high-low hem

A high-low hem is higher in the front than in the back. The split hem is a great opportunity to try a high-low hem because the split accommodates the length difference perfectly. See how to sew it in Chapter 19 (page 179).

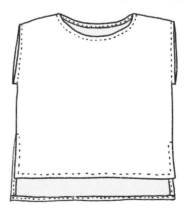

box dress

This is just about the simplest dress you can find, whether belted or worn loose. Depending on the fabric, you can tailor it to many occasions: A fancy dress in dark raw silk noil, belted, with simple jewelry; or as a floaty summer layer for a picnic, made up in cotton gingham with a split hem.

1. Gather the front body, back body, and dress extension pattern pieces. As noted on the pattern piece itself, line the dress extension piece up with the crop line on the front body and back body pieces, and tape them together—you're getting ready to cut one front and one back piece, each on the fold.

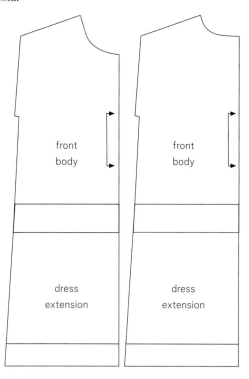

2. You can adjust the dress length at this point by cutting and overlapping pattern parts to shorten, or by adding more paper in between them to lengthen. If you do this, use a ruler to redraw the side lines so they're nice and straight.

3. Next, you may want to measure the circumference of the pattern at hip level, to make sure you have the amount of ease that you like. You'll probably want 5"–6" (13–15 cm) or more of ease at the hips. You may want to experiment with grading between sizes here to flare the box dress out a little wider at the bottom than at the top.

4. Refer to pages 80–81 in Chapter 7 to finish your dress by sewing the arm openings, neckline, and bottom hem. The box dress is the same as the main box top pattern—just longer.

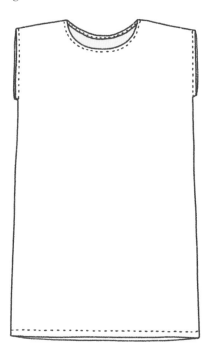

belt

Have a little extra fabric, and want to cinch in your dress at the waist? Make a belt! See Chapter 19 (page 182).

patch pockets

You can add patch pockets to literally anything, and definitely to the box top! Where you place your patch pockets is entirely up to you.

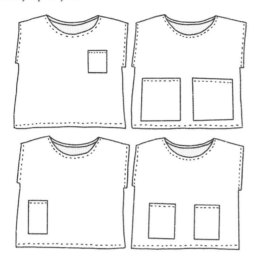

A good place to start for two patch pockets side by side (using the large patch pocket and regular length box top for reference) would be to measure 9" (23 cm) down from the center of the front neckline and 2" (5 cm) across from the center fold, and use that spot for the top inner corner of your patch pocket. That placement would look something like this:

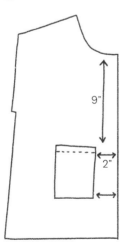

But maybe you'd like the pockets somewhere else: a little closer together, a little farther apart, a little higher, a little lower? The great thing about patch pockets is that they can be added after the top is finished. We recommend making your top, putting it on, pinning your prepared patch pockets to the top, looking in a mirror, and adjusting them until they're in the perfect place. See how to sew pockets in Chapter 19 (page 180).

extra-deep hem

An extra-deep hem is really beautiful on the box dress, or when working with thicker fabrics. It gives a high-end, couture look and feel to the garment. This style pairs well with the split hem hack techniques too. See instructions in Chapter 19 (page 179).

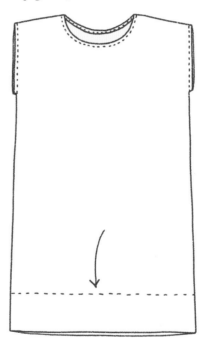

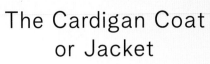

PART III

THE CARDIGAN COAT

- - - - - - - - - - - - -

The Cardigan Coat
or Jacket

Chapter 11

Cardigan Coat or Jacket

The ultimate versatile layer to make a dozen different ways, this is the kind of pattern we get really excited about. Maybe that's because the cardigan coat isn't your ordinary sewing pattern at all. It's more like a template, or a springboard—a carefully designed base waiting for you to take it and run with it. This is the kind of pattern you can know by heart, hardly needing the instructions after you've made a few. You can sew it ten different times and produce a totally different garment each time, and you can hack it nearly effortlessly just by following a scrap of an idea or letting the fabric take the lead. That's how we've been using it, sewing it again and again in all kinds of fabrics, trying things, experimenting with different sizes and fabric drapes, feeling like it's always new.

There is just one main pattern piece to trace from the pattern sheet in the back of the book: the combined front/back body. Follow the steps to make adjustments and find your way to a pattern that is personal to your body measurements (and your fit preferences and your life and your climate). Once you have this base, you can use it again and again. You will end up with two pattern pieces: the front body and back body.

If you want pockets, cut out two pocket pieces. There are three pocket shapes you can choose from. Or draw your own, or skip the pockets entirely. Up to you!

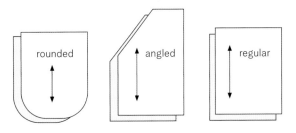

More than official variations, this pattern has options, lots of them. Sew a crop-length cardigan, a mid-length cardigan, or a long coat. Wear it loose and casual, belt it (page 182), add buttons (page 184), add a tie (page 183). Add pockets—rounded pockets, angled pockets—collar options, closure options. Try lots of different materials using this pattern as a base. You might also find that you like your sleeves cut separately, so try a sleeve that has just one seam on it, down the underarm—see page 121 for that.

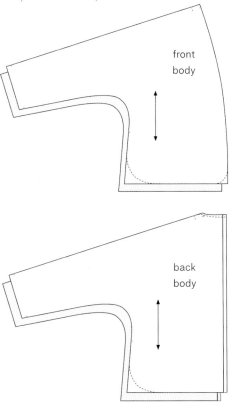

measurement chart and sizing for cardigan coat

Because ease is so subjective, the size you choose is ultimately up to you, and it all depends on how much roominess you'd like in your finished cardigan coat. It's designed to be worn with a range of 9"–15" (23–38 cm) ease at the bust/chest to achieve easy fit and layering possibilities, so that's what our size chart is based on.

Cardigan Coat Size Chart

Size Number	Size Letter	Bust Finished Garment Circumference		Bust (for recommended ease)	
		inches	cm	inches	cm
1	S	46.5	118	32–38	81–97
2	M	50	127	35–41	89–104
3	L	53.5	136	39–45	99–114
4	XL	59.5	151	45–51	114–130
5	2XL	65	165	50–56	127–142
6	3XL	70.5	179	56–62	142–157

You may want to fine-tune or tweak your ease, depending on what kind of garment you want to make. If you're making your garment as a cardigan, we recommend you sew your straight size, allowing about 9"–15" (23–38 cm) of ease relative to your chest/bust circumference. If you're making your garment as a coat, you may want to think about sizing up to allow for 14"–20" (35.5–51 cm) of ease to give you even more room for layering and movement with thicker fabrics. (Do you like to wear sweaters under your coat like we do? This choice may be for you!)

fabric types

The cardigan coat is designed to work for mid-weight to heavyweight woven fabrics or not-super-stretchy knits in a range of different drapes and feels. Your creativity in fabric choice is what will bring this pattern to life. We definitely recommend making a wearable muslin with a mid-weight nonstretch woven fabric that isn't too hard to work with—like about a 5 oz/yd^2 (170 gsm) linen, raw silk, or cotton—to see how this pattern works on your body. (See our tips for making a muslin on page 66.) Once you've gotten the fit and your adjustments where you'd like them, you'll find that the construction is pretty simple, so you can be pretty adventurous with your fabric.

We've made cardigan coats in all sorts of different fabrics, and we love seeing how the fit changes with each. Every fabric drapes differently, and therefore every fabric reacts to ease differently too—you might try going up or down one size number in different fabrics. For example, a cardigan coat in the exact same size on your exact same body will look totally different in drapey linen versus thick wool—both are cool options, one flowy, the other more structural. Read through Chapter 12 if you're planning to sew a quilt coat.

fabric amounts

The following charts show the recommended amount of fabric for each variation. The amounts are generous to allow for shrinkage from washing—you might be able to use less.

Cardigan Coat, Crop Fabric Requirements

Size Number	Size Letter	45" wide (yds)	115 cm wide (m)	60" wide (yds)	150 cm wide (m)
1	S	2.3	2.1	1.8	1.6
2	M	2.5	2.3	1.9	1.8
3	L	2.7	2.4	2	1.8
4	XL	2.8	2.5	2.1	2
5	2XL	2.9	2.7	2.6	2.4
6	3XL	3	2.8	2.8	2.5

Cardigan Coat, Mid Fabric Requirements

Size Number	Size Letter	45" wide (yds)	115 cm wide (m)	60" wide (yds)	150 cm wide (m)
1	S	2.6	2.4	2.1	2
2	M	2.8	2.6	2.3	2.1
3	L	3	2.7	2.4	2.1
4	XL	3.1	2.8	2.5	2.3
5	2XL	3.3	3	2.9	2.7
6	3XL	3.4	3.1	3.1	2.8

Cardigan Coat, Long Fabric Requirements

Size Number	Size Letter	45" wide (yds)	115 cm wide (m)	60" wide (yds)	150 cm wide (m)
1	S	3.1	2.8	2.6	2.4
2	M	3.3	3	2.7	2.5
3	L	3.4	3.1	2.8	2.6
4	XL	3.5	3.2	2.9	2.7
5	2XL	3.7	3.4	3.4	3.1
6	3XL	3.8	3.5	3.5	3.2

If your fabric is preshrunk (like boiled wool, or an existing quilt), you can use about 10% less length than shown in the chart. You will also need some bias tape or similar:

- *For Hemmed Edges*: 12" (30.5 cm) of 1"–1 1/2" (2.5–3.8 cm) wide bias tape, twill tape, ribbon, or similar for finishing the back neckline.
- *For Bound Edges*: 5 yd (4.6 m) of 3/8" (1 cm) wide double-fold bias tape, which is 1 1/2" (3.8 cm) wide unfolded. The exact length of bias tape you will need depends on how long your cardigan coat is and which size you're using.

some options for using less fabric

cut the back piece on the fold

If you have very wide fabric (like a quilt), are cutting one of the smaller sizes, or if you shorten the arms, you might be able to cut the back piece on the fold—to find out, try laying your pattern piece on your folded fabric. If you do this, you will want to remove 1/2" (13 mm) from the center back of the pattern piece, since it's no longer needed for the center back seam allowances. There is a mark on the pattern for this: You can trim off the excess, or fold it back, or just align the fold of the fabric with the line marked "Cut on Fold Line for Back" instead of on the regular center back line. Then, skip the step where you sew the center back together, but do everything else the same way as described in the sewing instructions.

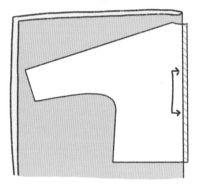

cut the sleeves separately

See page 121. Depending on the width of your fabric and front/back body pieces, choosing to cut sleeves separately could get you into a range where you can cut on the fold and/or fit the pattern pieces in much more tightly to use less fabric.

adjust the pattern, mock up the layout

If you haven't bought the fabric yet and want to buy as little as possible (very great for expensive fabrics), you can adjust the pattern pieces first, then lay out your pattern pieces on your work surface, pretending they're on top of imaginary fabric. Use your measuring tape or rulers to figure out exactly how much fabric you will need.

choose your finishing method

Take a look at your fabric, and think about how thick it is and how you think your sewing machine will feel about sewing it. If you fold a double-fold hem into the edge with your fingers, does the fabric feel very, very thick? If you do a few lines of test stitches, is your machine struggling to sew through the layers?

In medium-weight fabrics and even some heavyweight fabrics like canvas, it will likely still feel fine to use a normal double-folded hem. Great! But in thicker fabrics like wool or quilted fabric, a double-fold hem often doesn't make sense for this garment. You have some options. Would you like to bind your edges with bias tape or twill tape? This is a great choice for quilted fabrics, and for including some nice contrast along your edges. You'll find binding instructions in Chapter 12. Or would you rather still use a folded hem with a finished edge? Then use the option in this chapter to hem with a single fold.

trace your pattern

To begin, trace a copy of your size of the front/back body piece. Mark the lines for the front and back all on the same piece of paper; you're working with the front body and back body overlaid together. This is so you can make the adjustments once on the combined front body/back body piece, and then trace the individual front and back pieces.

Your tracing will look something like what is shown in the illlustration, just varied a bit based on which size you use.

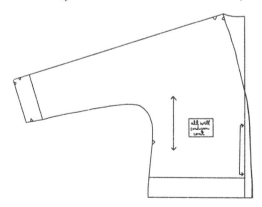

pattern adjustments

Even if you don't usually make pattern adjustments, you might want to here. This pattern is specifically drafted with just one arm length for all sizes, so you might want to take a look at the arms at the very least. Gather a pencil/marker, some scissors, some extra paper, and a ruler. Before you cut your fabric, these instructions will guide you through adjusting the pattern to fine-tune it to fit you.

Adjust length: The pattern is drafted to be about hip length for someone who is 5'3" (160 cm). If you are much taller than this, or if you want your jacket to be more cropped or longer, you will need to decrease or increase the length of the pattern piece. For reference, we recommend adding 3" (7.5 cm) for a mid-length cardigan or 7" (18 cm) for a long one. You might wish to add even more length if you're tall. To adjust the paper pattern, cut the pattern at the lengthen/shorten mark on the pattern piece, and either spread the pieces apart to the desired length and tape in more paper (to add length) or overlap the pieces (to remove length). Use a ruler to draw a new, smooth line to reconnect the sides of the pattern, following the slight taper at the side of the pattern.

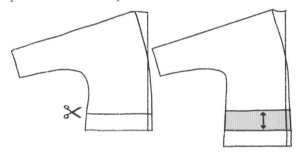

Lengthen or shorten sleeves to fit you: Arm length is mostly tied to your height, not your body circumference. So, with this pattern we're trying something different: The sleeve length on the pattern is the same for all sizes, just to give you a place to start. Adjust the pattern to fit your arms (and your preferences). If you sew the pattern without adjusting anything, your finished garment's sleeve will end up 26.5" (67.3 cm) long. So let's adjust:

- How long should your sleeve be? We need to find the measurement from the base of your neck to wherever you'd like your sleeves to hit. Use a flexible measuring tape and drape it along your shoulder and arm. (You can also use a piece of twine and measure that with a ruler.) We recommend measuring to bracelet length (mid-wrist), but you might prefer sleeves that reach all the way to your hands. Write your desired finished sleeve length down on the pattern.

- Unless your arm length happens to be 26.5" (67.3 cm), cut the pattern piece at the lengthen/shorten line to adjust. Add or subtract enough length to reach your measurement. For example, say you want your finished sleeve to be 28" (71 cm) long—you'd then be adding paper to lengthen your pattern by 1 1/2" (4 cm).

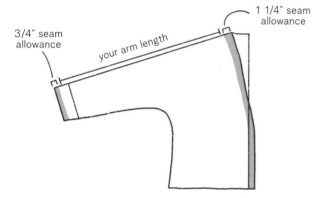

3/4" seam allowance

your arm length

1 1/4" seam allowance

TO LENGTHEN SLEEVE: Cut the pattern on the arm lengthen/shorten line, then add some extra paper under the pieces and spread the ends of the sleeve pattern apart until your sleeve is the desired length. Tape the new paper section in place and extend the side edge lines of the sleeve pattern to join the pieces.

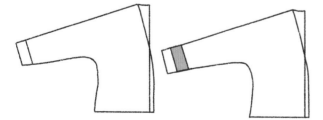

TO SHORTEN SLEEVE: Cut the arm pattern on the lengthen/shorten line; then overlap the cut ends of the sleeve on each other until your sleeve is the desired length. Tape the pieces together. Redraw the side edges of the sleeve to join.

- Finally, measure your pattern piece's arm length again—just to double-check. The whole top line of the sleeve should measure the same as your arm length, plus 2" (5 cm) for seam allowances.

Widen Arm/Wrist: The wrist of the pattern is tapered slightly. You may like a little more or a little less ease here, depending on the fit you're looking for and the fabric you choose. To widen the wrist opening, add some extra paper under the wrist and arm and tape in place. Draw a line to extend the wrist to the width you'd like, adding your extending line to the *bottom* of the wrist. Using a ruler, smoothly connect your new wrist endpoint to the underarm right at the spot where the underarm begins curving.

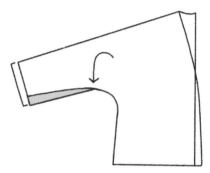

Once you've made all your adjustments on your paper pattern, trace out new front and back pattern pieces individually so that you have one of each. Now it's time to make a quick test version to check out the fit before you cut into your main fabric. See Chapter 6 on page 67.

fit guidelines

Here are some things you might want to think about as you assess your test garment, or sew through the pattern the first time:

LENGTH: You can sew the cardigan coat at the cropped length, or lengthen it to more of a hip length, depending on your own height and what kind of coat you're looking for. You could even make it longer for more of a duster look. The length here is very subjective and you're free to tweak it to your heart's content. No rules!

EASE: This coat is designed to be boxy and oversized, a coat that hangs a little bit away from the body. This will change dramatically depending on the fabric you select, but the intended fit is meant to have a good bit of positive ease.

ARMS: You will really want to pay close attention to the arms when you try on your test garment, especially being mindful of whether you want to wear bulky clothes under your coat. The happy middle between roomy and fitted is the goal here, which looks different for everyone. You want to check for a full range of movement, sleeves that feel like they're the right length (whatever that means to you), and nothing too poofy. Don't be afraid to adjust the arms to get them just right for you, lengthening/shortening and widening/narrowing as needed.

sewing instructions

cut your fabric

1. Cut your fabric. You want to end up with one left side and one right side of each piece, when the right (outer) side of the fabric is facing up. If you cut from a folded-in-half piece of fabric, this will happen naturally, but if you're cutting one layer at a time, flip over the pattern piece (so your writing is underneath) when you cut your second front and second back. Cut two front body pieces, two back body pieces (unless you're cutting on the fold), plus a pair of pockets if you'd like them. Then find or make your bias tape—you need about 12" (30.5 cm).

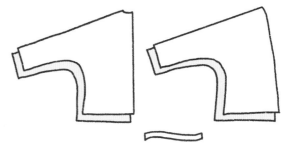

finish and sew center back seam

2. Finish the edges of the two front body and two back body pieces separately along the top seams and the sleeve/side seams, using the finishing method of your choice (serger, zigzag stitch, pinking shears). Finishing will not be pictured in the following illustrations.

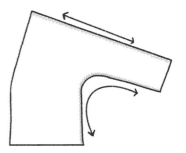

- -

TIP! If you're using a knit fabric or a tightly woven washed wool, you might not need to finish your inner seams at all. These fabrics don't tend to unravel in the same way other fabrics do.

- -

3. Finish the center back body raw edge on both pieces, using the finishing method of your choice. *Finishing will not be pictured in the following illustrations.* (If you cut the back body piece on the fold instead, you can skip to step 5.)

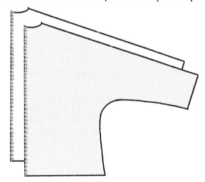

4. Line up your back body pieces with right sides together. Pin in place, and sew using a 1/2" (13 mm) seam allowance. Press seam open well. Now your back body is one large piece. *This center back seam will not be pictured in the following illustrations.*

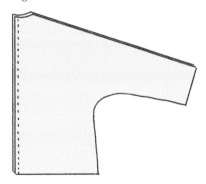

5. *Optional*: Staystitch along the curve of the back neckline, 1/8" (3 mm) from the edge, so it doesn't stretch out of place.

- -
TIP! Staystitching is a line of stitches sewn near a fabric edge (approximately 1/8" [3 mm] away) that may stretch as you you handle and sew it, like a curved or bias-cut edge. It serves to strengthen and stabilize the vulnerable edge. You can use your normal stitch length. The staystitching is hidden in the seam allowance, so it will not be visible in your finished garment.
- -

shoulder and side seams

6. Line up one front body piece with the back body, right sides together. Pin in place. It's best to match them up by laying the pattern pieces down on a flat surface to make sure you're aligning them accurately.

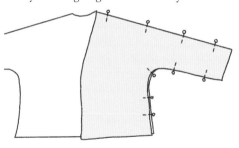

7. Sew the top shoulder seam using a 1/2" (13 mm) seam allowance, starting at the sleeve wrist opening, sewing toward the shoulder. Sew the shoulder seams to the dot on the pattern piece, 1 1/4" (3 cm) away from the edge of the shoulder, unless you want to bind your edges instead. In that case, follow the instructions in Chapter 12, starting with trimming seam allowances in step 2 on page 117. Press seam open.

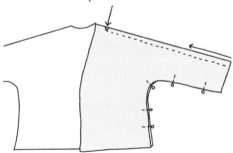

8. *Optional*: If you want a split hem, make a mark 3" (7.5 cm) above the bottom edge of the body pieces. This is where you will stop sewing for your split hem.

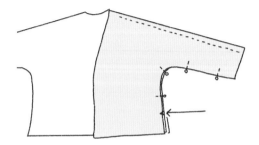

9. On the front body/back body you pinned together, sew the arm and side seam using a 1/2" (13 mm) seam allowance, starting at the wrist opening, sewing toward the armpit, then down the side seam. (Stop sewing at the spot you marked if you're making a split hem.) Press seam open using a sleeve roll or rolled-up towel.

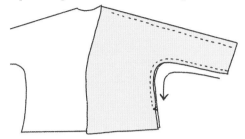

10. Repeat steps 6–9 for the other front body piece. Layer it over the other side of the back body piece with right sides together and pin.

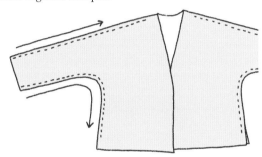

11. At this point, try on the garment and look in a mirror, paying attention to a few critical points. Keeping in mind that they'll change some when finished: Do you like where the wrists are hitting? How is the neckline falling? Does the length feel good at the hem? Trim or adjust any of the raw edges of your garment.

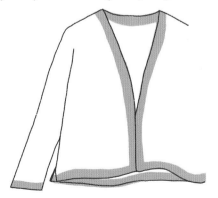

finish wrists

12. Finish wrists with a double-fold hem: Press the raw edge of one wrist opening 1/4" (6 mm) toward the wrong side; then press 1/2" (13 mm) again to prepare a 1/2" (13 mm) hem. If your fabric is too thick for this treatment, see the box below for single-fold hem instructions.

13. Sew with the sleeve right side out, and your presser foot inserted into the tunnel of the sleeve, so you can stay neatly along the folded edge as you sew. Edgestitch close to the edge of the fold all the way around to hem the wrist opening. Repeat for the other sleeve.

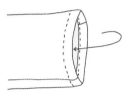

SINGLE-FOLD HEM, FOR THICK FABRIC

- Finish the raw edge of the wrist opening using your preferred method (serger, zigzag, pinking shears).
- Press the finished edge in toward the wrong side using a 1/2" (13 mm) seam allowance.
- Edgestitch all the way around the wrist opening, near your finished edge. When you sew, make sure your seam allowances are pressed open. Repeat for other sleeve.

---

finish back neckline

14. You will be finishing the back neckline and the front neckline edges of the cardigan coat separately. Let's start with the back neckline. You will need a 12" (30.5 cm) long, 1"–1 1/2" (2.5–4 cm) wide piece of bias tape, twill tape, or soft ribbon. Note: 1" (2.5 cm) is a good width for twill tape and ribbon; 1 1/2" (4 cm) is better for bias tape. If you are using pre-made double fold bias tape, it should be about 3/8" (1 cm) wide.

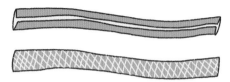

15. Lay your open bias tape or twill tape with right sides together along the length of the back body neckline, lining up the raw edge of the tape with the raw edge of the back neck. Find the center of the tape and line the center up with the center back seam. Pin in place.

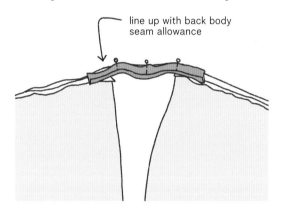

line up with back body seam allowance

16. Sew the tape to the neckline with right sides together, using a 3/8" (1 cm) seam allowance. Begin and end your line of stitching at the spot where the shoulder seams intersect; don't sew any farther. You will be sewing the tape to the seam allowance of the back body piece. Make sure that your front body seam allowances are still open and folded pointing down.

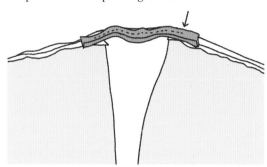

17. Press the seam allowance and tape up and away from the garment. Edgestitch the tape on the right side of the back body to the seam allowance, close to the fold, sewing only along the part of the tape that was sewn to the back body, not the free ends.

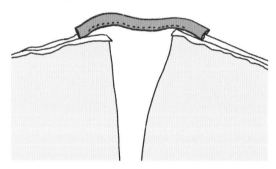

18. Flip your garment over and fold the tape and seam allowance over to the wrong side of the neckline so the tape is fully on the wrong side, not wrapping over the top of the seam. Position it so there's a thin line of the main fabric showing along the top of the tape. This helps ensure that your tape will not be visible from the right side of the garment. Pin in place.

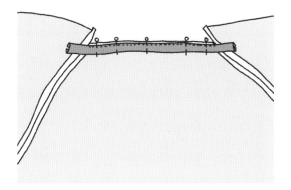

19. Edgestitch the tape along its bottom edge, beginning and ending your stitching at the shoulder seam intersections, leaving the edges free and unsewn.

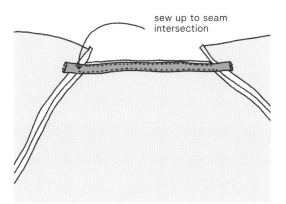

sew up to seam intersection

hem front neckline edges

20. Now finish the front edges of the neckline. To do this, make a double-fold hem in the front neckline, encasing the free ends of the bias tape you used to finish the back neck in the fold. Start by pressing one front neckline edge toward the wrong side 1/4" (6 mm), then fold again 1" (2.5 cm) to make a 1" (2.5 cm) wide hem. If your fabric is too thick for double-fold hems, see the box on page 112 for single-fold hem instructions.

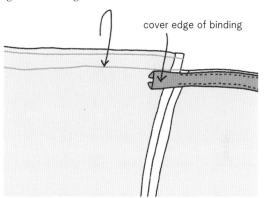

cover edge of binding

21. Pin in place, making sure that the front shoulder seam allowance is folded nicely down and the end of the tape from finishing the back neck is tucked neatly into the fold.

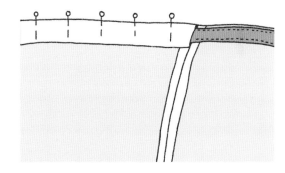

22. Sew a line of stitching along the top edge of the front neck hem on one side to tack it down (it should run right alongside the shoulder seam), then edgestitch along the fold to sew the front neckline all the way down to the garment's bottom edge. Use lots of pins and pressing.

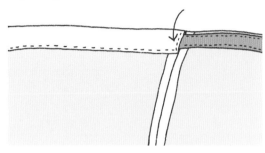

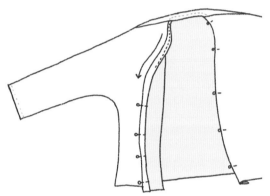

23. Make a double-fold hem on the neck of the other side of the front in the same way, being sure to tuck in the back neck's tape end, sewing all the way down to the garment's bottom edge. Remember to use lots of pins and pressing to keep the 1" (2.5 cm) hem tidy along the front neck.

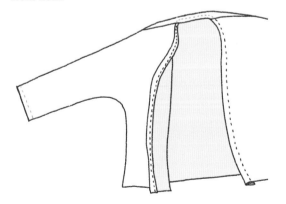

SINGLE-FOLD HEM, FOR THICK FABRIC

- Finish the raw front neckline edges using your preferred finishing method. (You don't need to finish the back neckline raw edge.)
- Finish the back neckline with binding, according to the instructions.
- Press the finished front neckline edges 1" (2.5 cm) toward the wrong side. (You might need to squeeze your extra tape from the back neckline in a little more to be covered by it.) Pin in place.
- Edgestitch near the finished edge all the way down the front neckline edges.

finish bottom hem

24. First, sort out the split hem, if you are using one. Repeat these steps on each side:
    a. Unfold the side seam allowance of the garment so that the split hem is lying flat and the wrong side of the garment is facing up toward you. Re-press the side seam open, making sure the seam allowance stays even at 1/2" (13 mm) along the split edges.

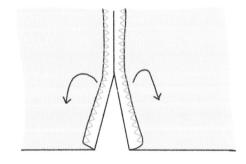

b. Starting from the bottom of the garment, edgestitch about 1/8" (3mm) in, close to the finished edge of the left "leg" of the split hem, up to just above the intersection where the split is joined.

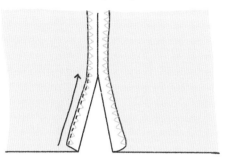

c. With the needle lowered, pivot to sew across the pressed-open seam until your needle is lined up with the finished edge of the right "leg" of the seam.

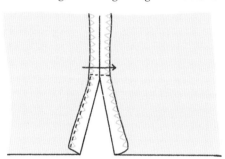

d. With the needle lowered, pivot to edgestitch down the right "leg" of the split to the bottom of the garment.

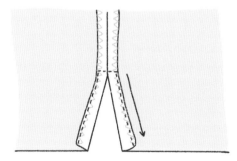

25. Finish the bottom hem of your cardigan coat using a double-fold hem: To do this, press the raw bottom edge up 1/4" (6 mm) toward the wrong side, then press the edge 1" (2.5 cm) up. Pin in place. (See the box below if fabric is too thick for a double-fold hem.)

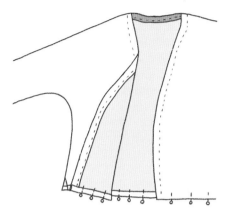

26. Edgestitch near the edge of the fold all the way around the bottom hem.

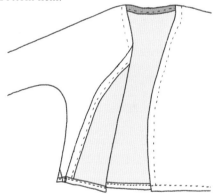

SINGLE-FOLD HEM, FOR THICK FABRIC

- Finish the raw bottom edge using your preferred finishing method (serger, zigzag stitch, pinking shears).
- Press the finished raw bottom edge up 1" (2.5 cm) toward the wrong side.
- Edgestitch near the edge of the finished edge all the way along the bottom hem. If you did not make a split hem, take care that your seam allowances are pressed open when the edgestitching tacks them down.

---

add pockets and finish

If you don't want pockets, that's fine too. In that case, you're done. Hooray!

27. Choose your pockets: There are two options that work well with this version of the cardigan coat—the regular pocket (rectangle-shaped) and the angled pocket (with the angle cut). (Pockets with rounded edges work best with the bias binding method found in Chapter 19, page 173.) Choose which shape you like for your project. It's up to you! Cut two pockets of your choice, making sure to cut them mirrored if you choose the angled pocket, since you need one for your right hand and one for your left.

28. Start by finishing all of the edges of each pocket piece, using your preferred finishing method: serger, zigzag stitch, or pinking shears. *(In the following illustrations, finishing will not be pictured, and we will show one of each type of pocket as an example. You will make a matching pair.)*

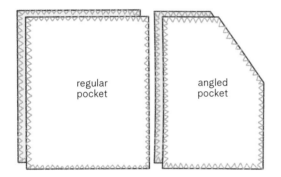

29. For rectangle pockets, press 1/4" (6 mm) of each side of the pocket toward the wrong side; then press 1/4" (6 mm) of the bottom edge of the pocket toward the wrong side. If you're making the angled pocket, press 1/4" (6 mm) of all of the edges *except* the angled edge toward the wrong side. Start with the sides, then press the top and bottom. Repeat for other pocket.

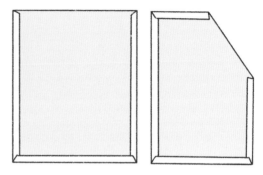

30. Press 1/4" (6 mm), then 1/2" (13 mm) of the top edge (or angled edge) of the pocket toward the wrong side. Pin in place.

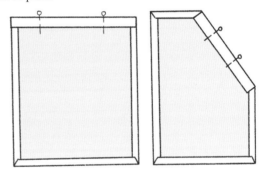

- -

TIP! If your fabric is thick and you'd rather do a single-fold hem here, go for it. You know what to do!

- -

31. Edgestitch along the edge of the fold all the way across the top (or angled edge) to hem the pocket opening.

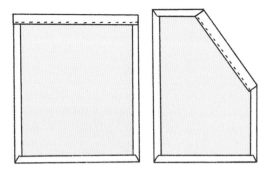

32. Put on your cardigan coat and stand in front of the mirror. Take one pocket and position it wherever feels best to you. Somewhere near where your waistline hits is pretty standard placement for the top of a pocket—you can look at other jackets for inspiration. Pin the pocket in place; then take off the cardigan coat and lay it flat on a table or the floor.

33. Look at how you positioned your pocket. Are the straight lines of the pocket parallel with the bottom hem and front neckline of the garment? This is your chance to reposition it before you sew. Align and re-pin as needed. Position and pin the second pocket and check its position also.

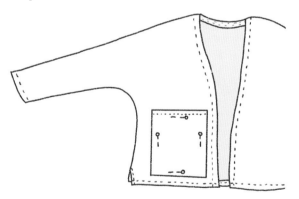

34. Go over to your sewing machine and topstitch the pockets to the front body pieces of the cardigan coat. Sew close to the edge of the fold. Start sewing at the top of one side and sew down, then pivot to sew the bottom, then pivot to sew up the second side. Do a little extra backstitching at the beginning and the end.

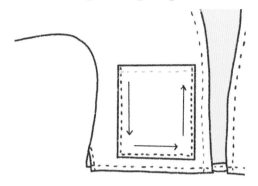

35. Yay! It's so close now. In fact, you could be done! Enjoy what you've made before making one final decision.

36. Take a moment now to think about your plan for closures. We aren't including specific closure instructions here, but if you want to add buttonholes, snaps, ties, a belt and belt loops, etc., now is the time to do it. See Chapter 19 for instructions for those. Finish the (optional) closures and then you're really done, hooray!

Chapter 12

Quilt Coat

There are few things more snuggly than a coat made out of a blanket. Quilt coats have long been a favorite of ours for their beauty, warmth, and uniqueness. Here's how to make one yourself. Bias-bound edges give the quilt coat a classic look (the binding echoes the way that quilts are traditionally bound), and it's also great for thicker fabrics like wool or prequilted fabric, where a double-fold hem would be too bulky. Looking for tips on sourcing old quilts and other thick quilt coat fabrics? Turn to page 204 in Chapter 23. Lots of thoughts! Lots of fun! It's always a particular challenge to transform something that is already impressive in its own right (like a quilt) into something new (like a quilt coat). We hope you will enjoy the creative process and make something you are proud of and will cherish for years and years. A quilt coat can become an heirloom just like a quilt can.

sewing instructions

prepare pattern and make adjustments

1. To begin, follow the steps in Chapter 11 (page 105) to lengthen the pattern as desired, and adjust sleeves and wrists if needed. If you haven't sewn a different version of the cardigan coat yet and are jumping into a quilt coat straightaway (yay!), we recommend making a quick test garment too. It will save you time in the end.
2. Because you're binding your edges instead of using a double-fold technique to finish them, you need to trim away part of the pattern. This is your chance to make a few design choices about your final quilt coat. If you made a test garment, you can make some educated decisions about whether or not you want to make these trims, but if you didn't make a test garment you can just go ahead and trim these off your tracing of the paper pattern.
    a. *Remove 3/4" (2 cm) at the end of each wrist.* Assess your test garment. Do you like where the wrists are hitting? You can leave them as is, or you can use a ruler to mark and trim off the seam allowance before proceeding. The sleeve length is drafted for bracelet-length sleeves, but all arms are different lengths, so decide if you like how it's working for you.

    b. *Trim 1 1/4" (3 cm) from the front and back neckline edges.* Use a ruler to mark and trim it off, unless you like the way the neckline is falling on you on the test garment. You may want to trim a little extra off, or you may decide you'd rather trim a little less, for a higher neckline. Pay close attention to the back neck—if you notice that it sticks up behind your neck, you can trim it down to a soft curve that lies nicely.
    c. *Finally, take off 1 1/4" (3 cm) at the bottom edge of the garment.* Use a ruler to mark, and then trim it now, unless you like where the cardigan coat is hitting on the test garment. If it feels good, leave it. Or you can trim off a few inches (7 cm) to make it shorter if you'd like.

cut your fabric

3. Once you have your pattern pieces customized to you, it's time to cut your fabric or quilt. You will need two front body pieces, two back body pieces (unless you're cutting on the fold), and bias tape or twill tape for binding. You can cut your pockets now or later too. If you're cutting an existing quilt or blanket, you might get creative with placement: some ideas on page 131.

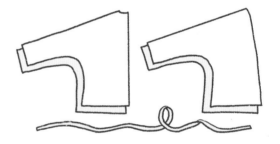

sew the body

4. Time to sew! Finish and sew the center back seam (unless you cut that piece on the fold), then sew the shoulder and side seams. (See detailed instructions in steps 3-10 on pages 108-109.)

5. Try the garment on and check the fit—see page 107 for guidelines. While you're trying it on, now's a good time to make any small adjustments to the neckline, overall length, or sleeve length, as desired—especially if you didn't make a test garment before. Even if you did, you might see a few things now that you want to tweak, given the particular drape of your material.

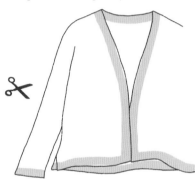

6. If you're happy with the fit, finish the shoulder and side seams as desired.

finish wrist openings

7. Finish wrist hems using double-fold binding. Go to Chapter 19 (page 173) for our master instructions about how to use this style of binding.

finish back neckline and hem

8. Bind the neckline, front edges, and hemline all at once, beginning and ending somewhere around the hemline. See the illustration below for the path you will take with your binding.

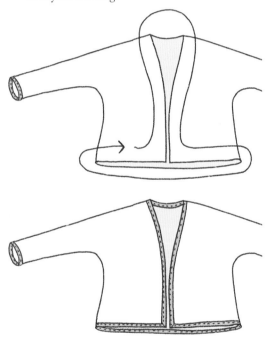

add pockets and closures

If you don't want pockets, that's fine too. Then you're done!

9. Choose your pockets: The rounded pocket is made especially for the quilt coat, because it's best finished with binding, but you can also use the rectangle pocket or the angled pocket. Whichever you choose, cut two. (If you choose the angled pocket, make sure to cut out two mirrored pieces so you end up with one right and one left pocket.)

10. Begin by binding all of the edges of each pocket piece with double-fold binding. *(Depending on which pocket shape you've chosen, it will look something like this. We'll show the angled pockets in the following diagrams.)*

11. Put on your quilt coat and stand in front of the mirror. Take one pocket and position it wherever feels best to you. Pin in place, then take off the coat and lay it flat on a table or the floor.

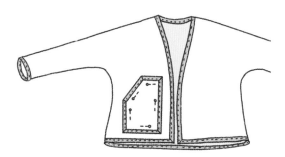

12. Look at how you positioned your pocket. Does it look wonky? Are the straight lines of the pocket even with the bottom hem or finished front edges of the garment? This is your chance to reposition it before you sew, to still have it near the comfortable spot you chose but to get it just right. Align and re-pin as needed. Pin your other pocket to the other side of your cardigan coat, matching the positioning of the opposite pocket.

13. Go over to your sewing machine and topstitch the pocket to the coat: Edgestitch close to the esdge of the binding all the way around except for the top opening (for the rounded or rectangle pocket) or the angled opening (for the angled pocket). Do a little extra backstitching at the beginning and the end. Repeat for the second pocket.

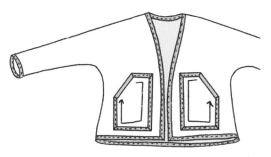

14. Do you want closures on your coat? See Chapter 19 for instructions for buttonholes, snaps, ties, belts, and belt loops.

finished

15. You did it! You made a quilt coat!

Chapter 13

Variations on the Cardigan Coat

The cardigan coat is designed with a simple soft neckline, straight boxed hems, and long sleeves, *but* that doesn't mean that's exactly how you have to make it every time. Once you have a base pattern that fits you well, you can vary the arms, hems, collars, and side shape to make dramatically different-looking jackets. Here are some of our favorite hacks and options.

cut the sleeves separately

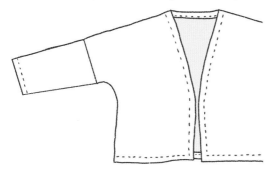

This is probably one of the handiest hacks. If you're short on fabric or want a slightly different look (an elegant dropped shoulder seam), cut your arm pieces separately. It's fun to play with the width and length of the sleeve too: Try an untapered, cropped sleeve for a dramatic look.

1. Finding the spot on the sleeve just before the underarm begins to curve, draw a straight line on your pattern piece from there to the shoulder line. Cut the pattern there, or trace the arms of your pattern onto a separate sheet of paper and just fold the sleeves back under the body of the pattern. Size 1 is shown in this illustration.

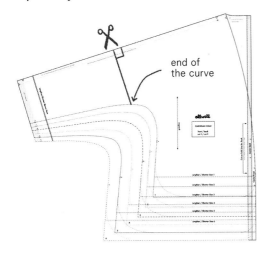

end of the curve

2. Add 1/2" (13 mm) seam allowance to the end of the new arm piece and the end of the body piece where you cut the arm piece off. Trim the 1/2" (13 mm) seam allowance off of the top edge of the arm piece—we will cut it on the fold instead of using a top seam.

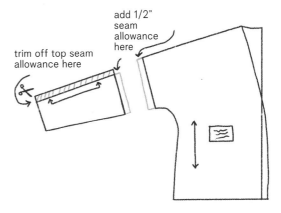

add 1/2" seam allowance here

trim off top seam allowance here

3. Place your pattern pieces on the fabric and cut them out. We recommend aligning the fold on the arm piece with the grainline, but you could also imagine that it was part of the body still and cut it on the same angled grainline as the body.
4. Finish the raw edges of the arm pieces as desired.
5. Sew, press, and finish center back seam if using. Sew the shoulder seams of the main body of the garment, then press seam allowances open.

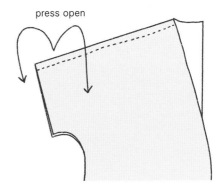

press open

6. Finish the raw edge of the arm opening (the raw edge of the arm piece should alreeady be finished). Line the arm opening and the arm piece up with right sides together, pin in place, and sew using a 1/2" (13 mm) seam allowance. Press the seam open.

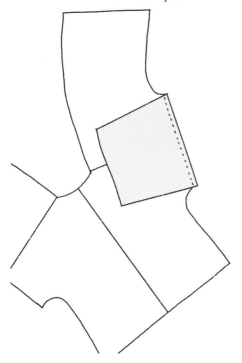

7. Sew the underarm and side seam as in the original pattern. Take care to match up the two seams that meet at the underarm as you sew.

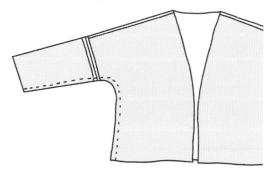

8. Finish the sleeve opening at the wrist normally, as in the pattern. Continue with the remaining instructions of the original pattern.
9. Hooray, you did it!

shawl collar

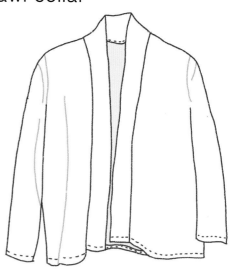

Want some extra warmth? With just one rectangle you can add a shawl collar. Decide whether you'd like a narrow shawl collar (which won't fold over on itself) or a wide shawl collar (which can fold in half like a robe collar or lapel).

1. Sew as usual to assemble the body of the cardigan coat, and sew the bottom hem and wrist hems. Sew the shoulder seams all the way up to the raw edge of the neckline, not stopping at the dot 1 1/4" (3 cm) away from the neckline.

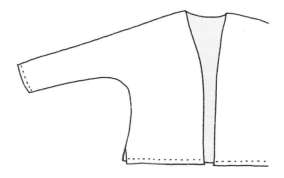

2. Measure along the full neckline curve from left bottom hem to right bottom hem.

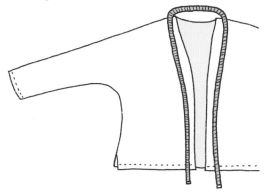

3. Cut a rectangle of fabric that is the length of your neckline curve plus 2" (5 cm), and either 7" (18 cm) wide (for a narrow collar) or 12" (30.5 cm) wide (for a collar that you can fold over). Mark the center of the rectangle with chalk or a pin.

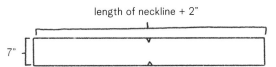

length of neckline + 2"

7"

4. Line up the rectangle with the neckline curve, right sides together. First, match the marked center of the rectangle with the center back seam, then pin down the collar, working out from the center toward the hems. You should have an extra 1" (2.5 cm) of fabric extending below the bottom hem on both sides of the front.

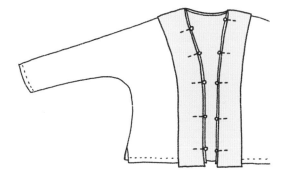

5. Sew the collar to the neckline curve using a 1/4" (6 mm) seam allowance.

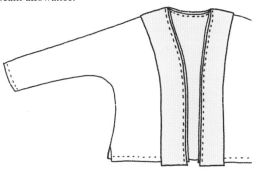

6. Press the collar and seam allowance up and away from the garment; then press 1/4" (6 mm) of the opposite (unattached) edge of the collar in toward the wrong side of the collar.

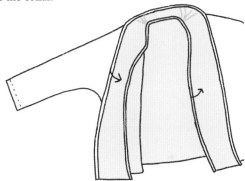

7. Next, press the entire collar in half so that the pressed 1/4" (6 mm) seam allowance ends up inside and positioned right below the seam that attaches the collar to the garment. Pin well from the right side to help ensure that your collar doesn't shift out of alignment while you sew it. Your seam allowance should now be hidden under the collar's fold.

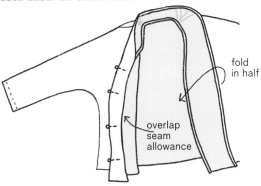

fold in half

overlap seam allowance

8. Starting at the back neck, stitch in the ditch (sew in the little ditch your earlier seam made, stitching right over your previous stitches) on the right side to secure the collar, making sure you're catching the underside edge of the collar with your stitches:

   a. From the back neck, sew down one side of your shawl collar, then sew down the other side.

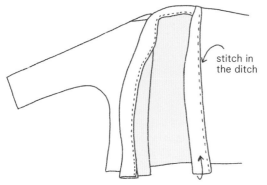

stitch in the ditch

   b. When you get to each bottom edge, fold the seam allowance in on itself so it nests inside the folded collar, then finish the seam to the bottom edge.

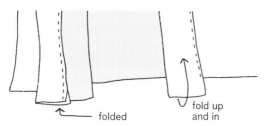

folded

fold up and in

9. Edgestitch the bottom edges of the collar to finish.

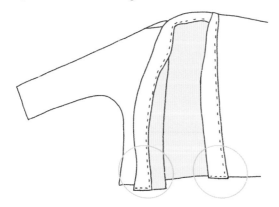

10. The shawl collar can be worn folded back or sticking up. It looks cool either way!

crewneck-ish front

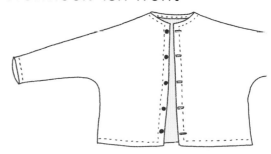

You can alter the cardigan coat pattern pieces to get a classic crewneck cardigan look. If you want to add buttons as seen in this diagram, see page 128 for directions.

1. Instead of cutting out the front body pattern piece, cut a total of four back body pieces. (It's easiest to use folded fabric to cut two at once. Take care with the right and wrong sides of the fabric.)

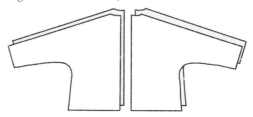

2. Find the trim line for the cardigan coat back neckline (the lower, lighter line) on the pattern, and trim one set of body pieces down to this line. At this point, you should have two sets of mirroring body pieces, one with the neckline trimmed and one without.

3. Use the trimmed neckline pieces as the back body and the untrimmed neckline pieces as the front body. Follow the instructions for the cardigan coat that begin on page 107, but in step 7, sew the shoulders all the way up the raw edge of the neckline. Stop after step 11, before you finish the edges.

sew all the way up to neck opening

4. Trim the two top triangles of only the front body pieces as shown in the diagram, the angles dipping down about 2 1/2" (6.5 cm). Start your cutting line at the point where the shoulder seam ends and the neck opening begins. Feel free to cut a little deeper than 2 1/2" (6.5 cm) if you like that look better. Try it on in front of the mirror and see! You can also cut at a gentle curve here, instead of the straight line of a triangle, if you want.

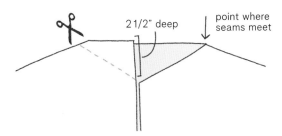

5. Finish using either the hemming method used for the cardigan coat (Chapter 11) or the binding method used for the quilt coat (Chapter 12).
   a. *Cardigan coat:* Finish the full top crewneck neckline, back and front, with the finishing method for the back neckline found in the cardigan coat instructions using bias tape or twill tape (Chapter 11). You will need a longer piece of bias tape, however long your neckline is plus at least 1" (2.5 cm) extra on either side. Sew the facing following the instructions in the cardigan coat pattern (Chapter 11) all the way around to the edges of the front neckline, then leave the edges raw; they'll get folded into the hem for the front edges of the cardigan.
   b. *Quilt coat:* Should be done the same as usual, with just a few extra corners to turn.
6. Finish the sleeves and front edges either with hemming or binding, tucking in the ends of the neckline binding as you go. You did it!

simple collar

Here's how to add a simple collar to the top neck of the cardigan jacket, giving it almost a chore coat look. It looks great in quilted fabric, or denim, or corduroy.

1. Follow steps 1–4 of the crewneck-ish front instructions in this chapter to alter the neckline of your cardigan coat, except this time cut all four pieces with the the top darker line for the neckline. It will look like this:

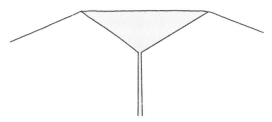

2. Finish the front raw edges of the cardigan jacket by either hemming or binding, using the instructions in the main pattern.

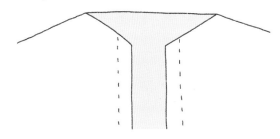

3. Cut a 22 1/2" by 5" (57 by 13 cm) rectangle from your main fabric. This will be your collar. (If you don't have enough solid fabric left, you can piece it together from smaller pieces; use a 1/4" (6 mm) seam allowance and press open on the wrong side.)

4. Pin the collar to the neckline with right sides together, leaving 1/2" (13 mm) of the collar hanging off each side beyond the finished edge. Depending on how you finished your front raw edges, you may have extra hanging off; trim the edges down to 1/2" (13 mm).

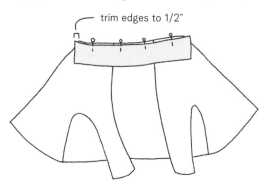

trim edges to 1/2"

5. Sew the collar to the cardigan coat with right sides together using a 1/4" (6 mm) seam allowance.

6. Press the collar and seam allowance both up and away from the garment.

7. Press 1/4" (6 mm) of the opposite raw edge of the collar toward the wrong side of the collar; then press the whole collar in half so that the edge of the collar extends just below the seam that attaches it to the coat.

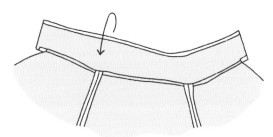

8. Pin well from the right side of the collar.

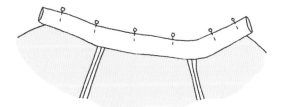

9. Stitch in the ditch (sew along the existing seam line) from the right side all along the collar, making sure you're catching the edge of the collar on the underside with your stitches—but before you begin, fold the raw edges under to tuck them into the collar.

10. Edgestitch each end to secure.

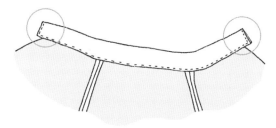

11. Yay, you did it! You made a simple collar. You can wear it folded down or sticking up. It looks really cool either way.

curved hem

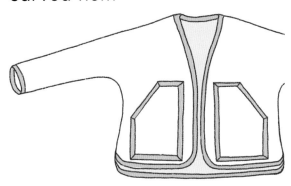

A curved hem is a beautiful and special detail that is not too difficult to add.

1. When you cut, you can use the dotted lines marked on the pattern piece to curve your hem. Or draw your own. Curve it at the front and sides, or just one or the other.

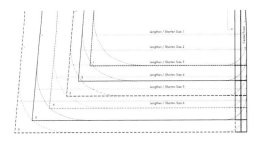

2. If you're binding your raw edges, follow the curve with your binding. At the side curve, maneuver your binding to follow the curve up to the side seam and then back down again. Take a little extra care at the side seam to make sure you keep things in line.

3. If you're hemming your raw edges, use a more narrow hem than prescribed in the pattern—try folding first to 1/4" (6 mm), and then again 1/2" (13 mm) toward the wrong side for a 1/2" (13 mm) hem.

wrap closure

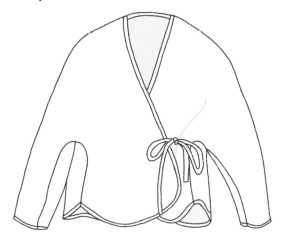

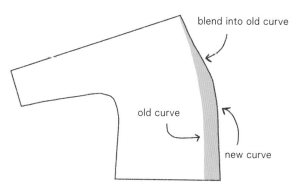

When sewn as designed, the ease in the cardigan coat pattern already allows a small amount of overlap for the two front edges, which means the pattern can already be worn somewhat wrapped without any alterations—but maybe you'd like an even more dramatic overlap or wrap. For a wrap look, you can add some secret ties to the inside and to the side that is partially covered, to help it stay in place. For a double-breasted look, you can add secret inner buttons. Here's how to make the wrap more pronounced:

1. Before you cut, put a separate sheet of paper under the front body pattern piece of the cardigan coat. Trace the shape of the front neckline, then slide the paper out a couple of inches (about 5 cm), however much more you'd like the front to overlap. Redraw the neckline to blend the existing pattern to the new front edge.

trace front curve and slide over

2. Sew normally, though your front edge may be a little trickier to hem. Work slowly and press well, and use pins to help you. You may want to use a narrower seam allowance if you're struggling with the 1" (2.5 cm) seam allowance in the pattern. If you're using the binding finishing method, it should be totally the same.

2. To make and attach the ties to the garment, see the "ties" section on pages 129–130.

buttons and snaps

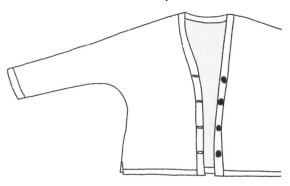

Cardigans and buttons—a perfect match! We recommend placing a button every 3"–4" (7.5–10 cm) and placing your top button right around the spot where the front edge begins to curve upward toward the neck, or just at—or above—your bust. Put on your cardigan coat and go stand in front of a mirror. Use pins or your fingers to overlap one side of the front neckline over the other and determine where the top closure would look and feel the best on your body. Each person's chest and body shape are unique, so this is a spot where you can decide what works well for you. You can use pins or safety pins to mimic buttons and wear the coat a little to see if it's comfortable.

It's up to you whether you want your buttonholes on the right or the left side. You don't need a button very close to the bottom edge of the hem, your bottommost button can be up to 4" (10 cm) from the bottom, the same spacing principle as for the other buttons. For a quick and simple closure, you can also just use a single button/buttonhole combo at the top button closure spot that feels best to you.

You can use a matchstick or something of a similar size to add space to your button stitching as you sew it, then slide it out once you're finished stitching.

You might also want to use snaps instead. (See tips for adding them on page 184.)

ties

If you hemmed your cardigan coat, you will want your buttonholes (as many as you'd like!) to fall within the hemline on the front edges if possible. Horizontal buttonholes are traditional for jackets (they're better for enduring stress), but vertical buttonholes will work great too. You may want to make your choice based on the size of your button and whether you used the 1" (2.5 cm) hem for your cardigan coat rather than binding. If a horizontal buttonhole can fit within the hem then go for it. If not, vertical buttonholes will still work great and will definitely fit within the hemline. If you used bias binding, the choice is yours. Sew your buttonholes into the 1" (2.5 cm) hem along the front edge if you hemmed, or along the front edge just beyond the binding. Mark your buttonholes on your fabric with chalk or another marking tool before you sew to plan where you will begin and end.

Once you've sewn your buttonholes (see page 184 for tips), overlap the buttonhole flap over the other flap and mark your button placement. You may want to place buttons for horizontal buttonholes a little farther in since the buttonhole will slide back and forth a little. Sew your buttons onto the garment with a needle and thread (or with your sewing machine if it has that capability). There needs to be some space between the button and your garment.

Ties are a simple and beautiful closure method for the cardigan coat. They add a lovely and almost whimsical touch to the final garment. They work especially well with the wrap-front hack (instructions on previous page), using up some of the ease and giving a different silhouette.

To add ties to your garment, first you'll need to make or gather the ties. For front ties you will need 20" (51 cm) total of tie fabric, and for the wrap you will need 40" (102 cm) total. You can use 1/2" (13 mm) twill tape for an effortless tie, or you can make your own ties out of the same or similar fabric as your garment. If you're using a heavy fabric for the garment, you will want to use a lightweight or mid-weight fabric in the same color to make your ties. See page 183 for constructing the ties themselves; then come back here to see how to attach them.

How to attach front ties:

Put on your cardigan coat and look in a mirror. Find the spot that makes the most sense for the two sides to connect together, where you'd place a single button if you had to. It will probably be around the spot where the straight front edges start to curve up toward the neck. Mark this spot with a pin on both sides.

- *Hemming*: Sew your tie to the wrong side at each pin marker on the cardigan coat. These stitches will be a little bit visible from the right side but if you use matching thread no one will be able to see them.
- *Binding*: Unpick your bias binding a tiny bit at the spot where you'd like your ties to be. Slide the unsewn end of the tie into the bias binding on the wrong side of the coat, then fold it back toward the edge of the garment and resew the bias binding and the tie together along the edge of the bias strip.

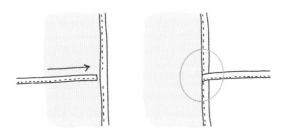

How to attach wrap ties:

You will use a similar method to the one used for front ties here, except you're going to insert two ties into both side seams as well. Look in a mirror and figure out how you'd like your cardigan coat to wrap. Mark with a pin the spot where you'd like your tie to be on both the front edges and the side seams, wherever feels comfortable for you. Treat the inner and outer ties a little differently.

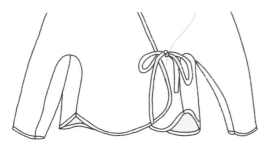

Inner Ties: These secret inner ties will help keep the underwrap (partly covered) side of your cardigan coat from shifting or drooping too much while you wear it. Sew one tie to the wrong side of the front edge of the underwrap side at the spot you pinned, using the methods given for front ties. Find the pin in your side seam for the underwrapped side and sew another tie to the side seam's seam allowance at the spot you pinned, until it is secure.

Outer Ties: These are the ties you will see on the outside. At the spot you pinned, sew one tie to the wrong side of the front edge that wraps over, using the methods given earlier for front ties. Find the spot you pinned at the corresponding side seam and seam-rip a 1/2" (13 mm) length. Slide the end of your tie into the side seam from the right side to the wrong side of the coat, just until the end of the tie is flush with the side seam's seam allowance, and restitch the side seam to secure. You should now have a tie hanging off the front wrap of the cardigan coat and a tie hanging out of one of the side seams on the right side. When tied, neither of the inner ties will be visible and both of the outer ties will be visible.

belts

We love the look of belting the cardigan coat. You might even already have a belt that would go with it. Want to sew one? Head over to page 182 to make a very simple fabric belt that will match your garment perfectly. If you want belt loops at the sides, follow the instructions for making ties (page 183), but make shorter ones. You might also want to add a second line of stitching along the edge of the tie that has no stitching, to get the classic belt loop look. Then sew them on in a little C shape on the sides of your garment.

hanging loop

This is one of our favorite features to add to the cardigan coat—we put a hanging loop in almost every one we make. Makes it really easy to hang your garment on a hook. See instructions in Chapter 19 on page 184.

flat-felled seams

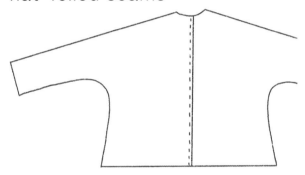

A flat-felled seam is a beautiful and durable finish for the center back seam. We love the look of it, and you will find flat-felled seams will come in handy for lots of other sewing projects too. Find the instructions in Chapter 19 on page 177.

make it reversible

You can make your cardigan coat reversible. Here are some ideas for how to do it:
- Flat-fell the center back seam (see Chapter 19, page 177), or cut on the fold.
- Bind all of your interior seams. This is the easiest way to get a reversible look. Choose a prequilted fabric or thick gauze with two different colors/tones, and choose a binding color you wouldn't mind showing

off. If you want a very neat finish, you can hand stitch down the side of the binding that sticks out so the binding lies flat against the garment.
- Use ties as closures.
- If you have just one or two or three buttonholes, you could stack two buttons to make a button sandwich—button, coat, button—so that you can button your garment with either side out.

special touches

Here are some other ideas for the cardigan coat you might want to consider:
- Add secret inside patch pocket(s). See patch pockets in Chapter 19 on page 180.
- Elbow patches. Ovals! Rectangles?
- Add cuffs to the sleeves.
- Make longer split hems to be extra dramatic. Try 5" (13 cm) to start. Or more, why not?
- Let the back panel of the coat be 1"–3" (2.5–7.5 cm) longer than the front (instructions for a high-low hem on page 179).
- Add a vent (like a big split hem) in the bottom of the center back seam, especially on a long coat.

If you're using a blanket or a quilt for your fabric, you can often incorporate elements from the quilt into your work.
- You might want to highlight a certain design element of the quilt by cutting very specifically—matching both front pieces. If the quilt has a border, you could line that up with the front edges of the coat.
- You can use the bound edge of the quilt for the bottom hem of your coat.
- You might feature certain design elements of the quilt on the pockets.
- This could be a good time to try to cut the back piece on the fold, so you have an unbroken expanse that will show off the quilt without a seam down the center.
- Play with the backing fabric of the quilt too. If you cuff the sleeves this will show. You could make the pockets match the backing color, etc.

prequilted fabric

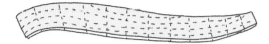

Prequilted fabric is an amazing way to get the quilted look without the work of quilting pattern pieces yourself. There is lots of it out there these days. Look for fabrics that aren't super thick or super stiff. You will know a nice prequilted fabric when you see it: you will want to wrap it around your body right away. With quilted fabrics, we recommend finishing the edges with binding for a classic look. You might look in unexpected sections of a fabric store, like the upholstery section. Another good source of prequilted fabric is to repurpose blankets or old quilts—more on that on page 204.

thick or fluffy fabric tips

Soft and squishy fabrics like sherpa and fleece, some wools, and all sorts of others can make amazing finished garments, but sometimes they're tricky to work with. Here are a few tips to help manage the fluff:

- Check the care instructions when you buy. Lots of puffy and fluffy fabrics need to be washed carefully or not at all.
- When you cut, check that the nap of the fabric is all going in the same direction. In some kinds of puffy and fluffy fabric, the nap is more exaggerated than others, so pay attention to it when cutting.
- Cut from the wrong side of the fabric. If your fabric is very fluffy, it may have a smoother wrong side. It will be easier to cut your pattern's shape more accurately on the back side of the fabric.
- Depending on the type of fabric, you may want to try a ballpoint needle so you don't damage your fabric.
- Did your machine come with a walking foot? It can make sewing squishy fabric much easier.
- Try using twill tape to bind. It's not very fussy and can help give a clean finish on the edges of your project. A double-fold hem can get very thick when using puffy and fluffy fabrics.

open top pouch

PART IV

ALL WELL BAGS

Carry what you need

small book bag

stand up pouches

small 3d book bag

fold-over pouch

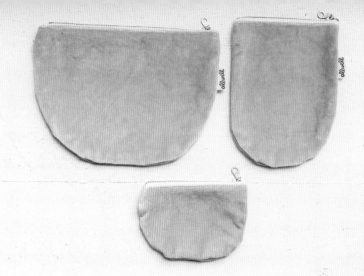

half moon zip set

flat pouch

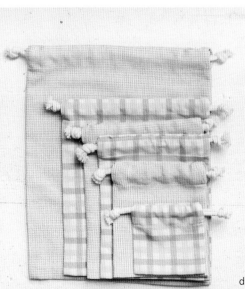

drawstring bag set

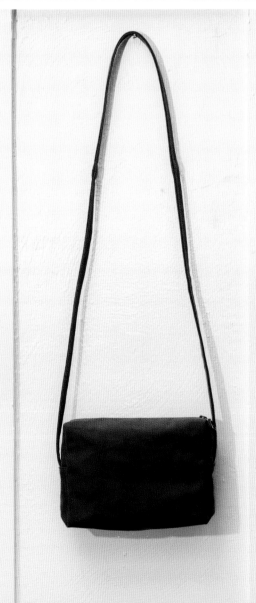

party purse

Chapter 14

Sewing Bags

We love simple bags—lots of them. A bag for every object! Bags to go inside other bags! The simpler, the better, in our opinion—utility and form meeting with durable materials and perfect proportions. A bag can be a daily companion in a way that a garment can't quite be. You don't typically wear the same clothes every single day, but you can use the same bag every day! So we want to make bags worthy of daily use, that are up to the challenge of whatever you need to carry. We love canvas, we love pouches made of scraps. We love snaps and straps, we love nice zippers, we love bags! Let's make some! But first, let's talk about all the little things that go into the process of planning and sewing bags.

really, it's all about fabric and materials

With bags (as with clothes), *it's all about the fabric, it's all about the materials.* If you love the fabric you're using to make a bag, you will probably love using the bag for a long, long time. A bag can be so simple: The fabric, the texture, the proportions, the gentle way it will wear and break in as you use it all work together to make it feel right. Take your time finding sturdy fabric, beautiful zippers that work well, the kind of straps you really want to use. Put the time and energy into sourcing your materials in your own way, within your own budget, in your own time. It will be worth it. In fact, the sewing might be the fastest part of the journey from idea to a bag full of all you need to carry.

The best fabric for a bag depends on how you plan to use it: soft cotton for pouches; thicker, stiffer material for totes; something with structure for bags that need to stand on their own. Scraps are great for soft bags, and we really like sturdy canvas or denim for almost any other bag.

a small note
What we don't like: Interfacing or lining. There's nothing wrong with these things, we just prefer unlined bags, so they aren't in our patterns. (You're welcome to hack the patterns to add them, of course.) We like bags that are made with fabric that is sturdy and stiff enough to hold its shape, and we like to bind with bias or twill tape, or leave seams artfully serged or zigzagged to finish.

sturdy bag fabric sourcing

It can be hard to find sturdy canvas for bags, and a little harder to sew it, but that sturdiness is what will make your bag really nice to use for a long, long time. We don't love interfacing, so we look for that structure in the fabric itself—that makes us really choosy about our canvas. Make sure to pay attention to the weight of your fabric when selecting a canvas. It is available in many weights and hands. We recommend using 10 oz/yd^2 (339 gsm) canvas and heavier, but anything above 12 oz/yd^2 (407 gsm) may begin to be difficult to sew on a standard home sewing machine. You have to find the sweet spot of fabric weight. *Cotton canvas* and *cotton duck* are two industry names for similar fabric—cotton duck has a higher thread count than canvas and a more drapey hand. Learning and experiencing the difference between different weights and varieties of canvas will help you find the kind you like best, so this is where shopping in person is somewhat critical. It's almost impossible to know for sure whether the canvas you are sourcing will arrive with enough stiffness to do what you need it to do. So many times we've thought we found what we wanted online and were disappointed by floppiness when it arrived. Just wanted to give you fair warning. Stiff fabric is what you're seeking for bag sewing.

There might also be other special bag fabrics you want to source, and in these cases online shopping is likely the only way to go and works pretty well, since specialty fabric sellers usually have a lot more detail available. For example, if you're sewing climbing or hiking gear, you might look up fabrics like Cordura, Dyneema composite fabric or Cuben Fiber, and other synthetic fabrics online, or you might be looking for leather or shearling from specialty stores like MacPherson, Tandy, or Springfield. Either way, it gets easier as you go along, but just know that sourcing good bag fabric can take time, and it's worth it.

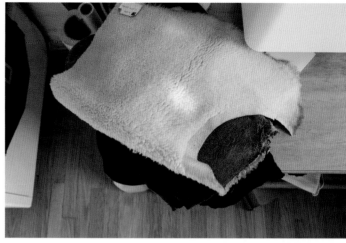
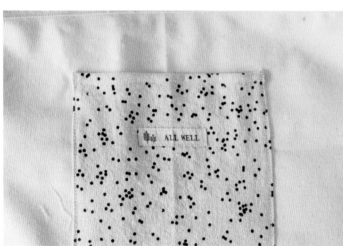
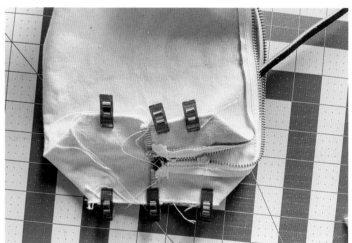

how to customize bags for you

Another good thing about bags is all the ways you can make them fit your life. You can size the bag for just what you want to carry. For example, Amelia often carries a notebook, pen, and book around, and it can be nice to have a small pouch just for them, to keep them safe when they're floating around within a bike pannier or tote. Amy uses a fold-over pouch as a snack pack for bringing food on walks. You could customize the strap on a party purse or 3D book bag so it hits *just right* for your height and body. Make your simple pouches super small or *wildly* oversized to play with proportion.

There are so many details you can add: loops to clip your keys to or a hang loop. A leather tab or extra stitching at the corners. A tag. Pockets! Extra straps and attachments: For example, do you use a bike or scooter or wheelchair to go places, where you might want to have your hands free? You could design little straps to attach a bag to a frame, handlebars, or seat. With bags, it can be nice to dream up new combinations that are super specific to your life.

pocket ideas for bags

We love pockets. Here are just a few ideas: Secret pocket! Padded pocket for your sunglasses! A zip pocket for important things! You might decide to design pockets specially sized for what you carry or add divider pockets to split up a bag into compartments. Or divide a patch pocket by sewing an additional seam vertically to split it into two pockets. Don't forget pockets-on-pockets (the double patch pocket!) as an option; also, if you size an interior patch pocket smaller than an exterior one, the seams will be hidden from the outside.

making your bags fancy

The word *fancy* might bring to mind some very specific and very elaborate vision of a bag, but to us *fancy* can simply mean attention to detail and material, and maybe a little extra time and care spent on the cutting and sewing. Here are a few fancy ideas—sort of general-purpose hacks you can add to many types of bags: Add a zipper pull, a leather tab or leather strap, reinforced seam intersections, or patch pocket tops with rivets. Add snaps (page 184) or grommets or rivets—they're all less tricky than you'd guess.

Bags often use such small amounts of fabric that it becomes more possible to be decadent. Make a drawstring bag or fold-over pouch set out of a very special silk or linen. Use a beautiful ribbon for the drawstring. For bags with zippers, we like plush shearling or buttery soft leather. Add your own surface designs to any bag's fabric after you cut the pieces and before you sew it. This works extra great with canvas. Because it is made from cotton, a natural plant fiber, canvas dyes very well and is excellent for surface design of all kinds like block printing, screen printing, marbling, and painting. Or you could add patches, or needle-turn appliqué, or embroidery. Abundance!

our best bag tips

- For anything with structure, sturdy fabric is a must! Floppy fabric means floppy bag.
- The quality of the materials in your bag matters a lot: the zipper, any bits of straps. If you look closely at the ready-to-wear bags you really love to use, you will likely notice nice zippers that work well, quality hardware, nice thick fabric. Those are the sorts of things you're looking for when you're making a bag yourself too—and unfortunately some of the bag supplies commonly available in sewing stores fall somewhat short, so you may have to go looking.
- If your bag will be used with a specific orientation, like a fanny pack or bike bag, think about how the pockets and zippers are placed in relation to your dominant hand.
- Bags are made to be heavily used, so sew them extra strong. This might mean trying out heavy-duty thread or reinforcing some seams of often-used pockets or straps.
- If you're making a couple of pouches to give as gifts, try batch sewing them. You can work on all of them at once by going one step at a time and finishing that step for each pouch before moving onto the next step. This often makes sewing multiples feel quicker.

Chapter 15

Simple Pouches

fold-over

drawstring bag

open top

Oh, the joy of having a place for everything. Bags like nesting dolls, little homes for things. Try an open top pouch for things you need quick access to, like a phone or notebook or computer, or try a fold-over pouch for containing soft things, or add a drawstring or flap to keep things secure. A bag for your earbuds inside a bag for your electronics inside your backpack, on your back. So cozy! To some it could seem a little over-the-top to have bags inside bags inside bags, but for us it is a truly happy feeling to tuck things away just so. You too? Making them yourself makes them that much more satisfying, that much more fine-tuned for exactly what they will hold. The bags in this chapter are perfect for just that.

These simple pouches are good for practicing your sewing skills—like sewing in a straight line, pivoting at corners, pressing a double-fold hem, and cutting and placing pattern pieces. And most of the dimensions don't need to be so exact—bags are very forgiving.

open top pouch for a phone, device, or journal

This is possibly one of the simplest things to sew and one of the *most* satisfying. Once you start making little pouches for all your favorite things, you won't be able to stop. Snack bag! Phone holder! Computer sleeve! Journal protector! Pen case! A sleeping bag for a doll! Making a custom-sized simple pouch is as easy as measuring an object—and we also have some suggested sizes for you to try too. The larger sizes are easiest to sew.

AMY: My favorite simple pouch I've made is a little phone caddy, sewn in ten minutes one day because I was wearing an outfit with no pockets (horror!) and wanted to listen to a podcast with my earbuds (back when my earbuds had a cord) while sewing. I stitched up a simple pouch, sized exactly to my phone from a scrap of canvas, added a quick twill tape strap, and I've been using the same phone pouch ever since for all my no-pocket days. It's times like that that sewing feels extra powerful— being able to meet an immediate need and make something simple and exactly right.

Open Top Pouch, Finished Sizes

	width (inches)	height (inches)	width (cm)	height (cm)
Small	4	6.5	10	16.5
Medium	7	9.5	18	24
Big	9.5	13	24	33

Fabric for Open Top Pouch

	45" wide (yds)	115 cm wide (m)	60" wide (yds)	150 cm wide (m)
Set of three	0.7	0.6	0.5	0.4

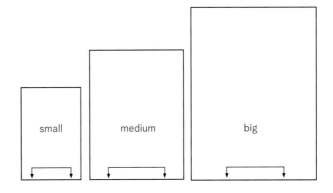

1. Cut fabric with the fold line of the pattern arranged on the fold. (Or make the pattern piece twice as big and cut your fabric flat.)

2. Fold fabric in half with right sides together. Pin each side, then sew each side with a 1/2" (13 mm) seam allowance.

3. Finish side seams and press well.

4. Snip a triangle off of the seam allowances on the open side of the pouch.

5. Fold down the top edge, pressing 3/8" (1 cm) down to the wrong side; then fold over and press 3/8" (1 cm) again. Pin in place. Make sure both side seam allowances are on the same side of the pouch when you tuck them into the hem.

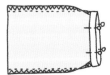

6. *Optional*: If you want a strap (like for Amy's phone caddy pouch), tuck it under your pressed hem where desired. Twill tape works great for this.
7. Edgestitch to sew a hem all around the top.

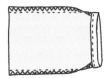

8. Flip the pouch right side out, and press one final time to make everything crisp. Yay, an open top pouch!

a strategy for making a custom size

1. Decide how big to make it. Place things you want to put in your pouch on your pattern paper, then draw a rectangle around them with a bit of padding—more extra space for thicker objects. You're looking to have enough so that when you put things in and the bag gets a bit more three-dimensional, everything will fit and slide in and out easily, but not be so loose that things fall out.
2. Draw a fold mark at the bottom of the pattern. Then add seam allowances: 1/2" (13 mm) to each side, 1" (25 mm) to the top. That's your pattern!

fold-over pouch

What do we put in fold-over pouches? Cords, soft things like face masks, kid or baby gear, or a snack pack with little bars and things to eat while on a walk or around town. Tote bag storage: so useful to keep things separated while carrying them around in a larger bag. Earphones with cords, and lots of stuff that's not rigid—sometimes a pen, and very flexible or smaller notebooks. In general, fold-over pouches are great for holding a bunch of small objects.

The fold-over pouch pattern pieces include a set of three. You can also hack the pattern to make them any size you'd like, of course—even really big. You could use this same concept to make a pillow or cushion cover. Here are the sizes, dimensions, and amount of fabric you will need to make them.

Fold-Over Pouch, Finished Sizes

	width (in)	height (in)	width (cm)	height (cm)
Small	5	6	13	15
Medium	6	7	15	18
Big	7.5	7.5	19	19

Fabric for Fold-Over Pouch

	45" or 60" wide (yds)	115 or 150 cm wide (m)
Set of three	0.6	0.6

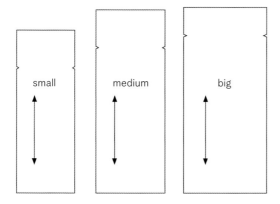

1. Trace the pattern (taking care to transfer notches), then cut your fabric.

2. Hem the shorter ends (these will become the opening of the pouch) by folding over 3/8" (1 cm) twice toward the wrong side. Pin, then edgestitch.

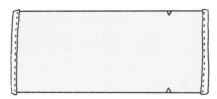

3. Flip so the right side is facing up; then fold the edge closest to the notches over with right sides together, so the fold line is at the notches.

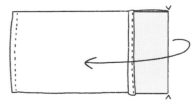

4. Fold the other edge up to almost meet the top fold, leaving about 1/8" (3 mm) of space. Pin in place.

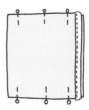

5. Sew the sides with a 1/2" (13 mm) seam allowance.

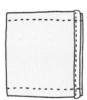

6. Finish the raw edges of the seam allowances; press well.

7. Turn it right side out for the big reveal. You did it—a fold-over pouch!

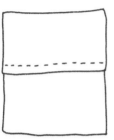

drawstring bag set

This set of six drawstring bags gives a lot of options. The smallest ones fit earbuds or an earbud case, personal toiletries, chapstick, small tampons or condoms, tiny hot sauce, mints, jewelry, coins, candies (sour Hi-Chew, integral to the writing of this book!), or gum—and whatever else you can dream up to put inside. Larger ones could be filled with books, or stuff you want to take with you to the beach, or the library, or work. Maybe a drawstring bag could be fun to pack delicate things in for a trip, or to fill with a gift for a friend.

This drawstring bag features a small, hidden bottom gusset, which you can leave out if you want. The bag still lies flat, but when it's filled it has a bit of room to stand up. Use the chart below to choose which size bag you would like to sew.

Drawstring Bag, Finished Sizes

	width (in)	height (in)	width (cm)	height (cm)
1	3.5	4	9	10
2	4.5	6	11.5	15
3	5.25	7.5	13.5	18.5
4	6	8	15	20
5	7	9	18	23
6	9	12	23	30.5

The chart below shows how much fabric you will need to make a full set of six drawstring pouches, although this is another great project to make out of fabric left over from other projects, instead of buying new.

Fabric for Drawstring Bag

	45" or 60" wide (yds)	115 or 150 cm wide (m)
Set of six	0.9	0.8

For a full set of six drawstring bags, you also will need 6.5 yards (6 m) of any small thin cord; this drawstring length recommended is enough for two strings that cinch the bag closed. If you like the look of just one drawstring, you can use half the amount. Those amounts are also for strings that don't stick out very far when the bag isn't cinched—if you want longer or shorter strings, go for it!

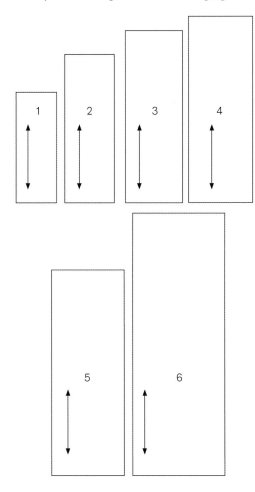

1. Fold your fabric in half with right sides together. Position the folded edge at the bottom.

2. Fold the bottom edge up toward the top by 1/2" (13 mm) and pin in place.

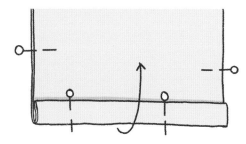

3. Measure down 2 1/2" (6.5 cm) from the top edge on each side, and snip a notch through both layers of fabric, staying within the seam allowance.

4. Sew a seam up one side, stopping just before you reach the notch marking. (The top parts are not sewn yet, to leave room for the drawstring channel.) Repeat for the other side.

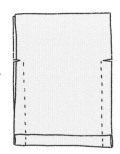

5. Finish the seams just up to the notches; then press the side seam allowances to one side and make sure your notches are still visible. Recut them if you need to.

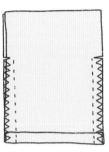

6. On the top unsewn part of each seam allowance, make a small double fold along the sides of the pouch and press well. Edgestitch for extra security. Do this four times, twice on each pouch side.

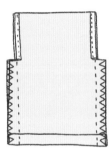

7. Hem both layers at the top edges by pressing each down 3/8" (1 cm), then 1" (2.5 cm) toward the wrong side. You will be making two separate channels for the drawstring to go through, two separate little tubes. Press and pin.

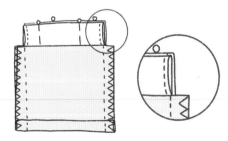

8. Flip your whole pouch out to the right side, tuck the side seam allowances toward one side and up under the hem, and then edgestitch the top hem all in one go, sewing along the bottom edge of the fold. Try to go for one big circle of stitches, without a large gap between the two drawstring openings on each side. And make sure your stitches tack down the side seam allowances.

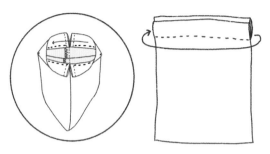

9. Time to add drawstrings—one is good, two (with knots/ties on opposite sides of the opening) are even better. Up to you! Thread the strings through the drawstring channels, using a bodkin or safety pin to help. Knot the ends together and trim.

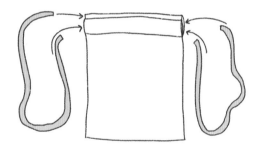

10. A drawstring bag! How cute! What are you going to keep in it?

Chapter 16

Book Bag

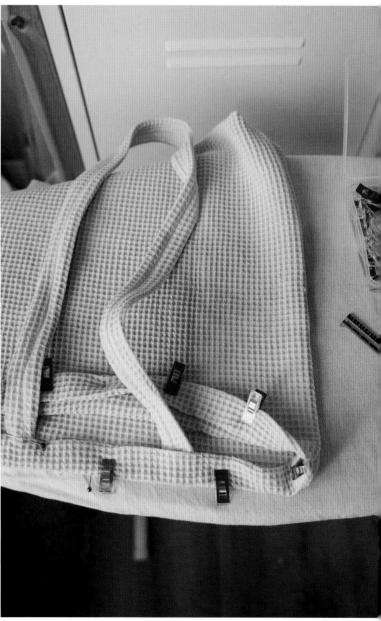

This simple tote will show off beautiful fabric and carry whatever you need to lug around. (In our case, usually books!) Make it 3D, to carry a little more, with just two extra seams. A quick sew, perfect gift, or wardrobe companion. (Match your tote to your outfit?) The possibilities are endless.

The sewing instructions show you where to add an extra bit of stitching if you want to make it three-dimensional; either way, start with two strap pieces and one bag piece, cut on the fold. Find them on the pattern sheet and trace out the rectangles.

The chart below gives the finished dimensions of the bags, not including the strap. The little one is quite small, perfect for gift giving, a tote for kids, or carrying a lunch.

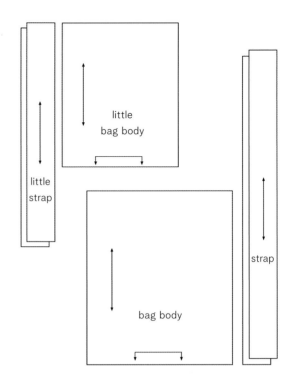

Book Bag, Finished Sizes

	width (in)	height (in)	depth (in)	width (cm)	height (cm)	depth (cm)
Little	11	13	–	28	33	–
Regular	14	16	–	35.5	40.5	–
Little 3D	10	12	2	25.5	30.5	5
Regular 3D	12.5	14.5	3	32	37	7.5

The strap is a bit longer on the regular-size bag; feel free to customize the strap length or size if you'd like. You can sew both a little and a regular size from just one yard or meter of fabric. We've made these in linen, cotton canvas, thin denim, and some squishy waffle knit found in a thrift store as a pair of old kitchen curtains. Up to you—this bag is one you can take in a lot of directions, depending on the fabric you choose.

Fabric for Book Bag

	45" or 60" wide (yds)	115 or 150 cm wide (m)
Both bags	1.1	1

Prepare straps

1. Fold the top long raw edge of the strap down 1/4" (6 mm) to wrong side of fabric and press.

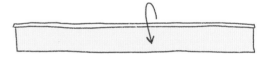

2. Fold the bottom long raw edge of the strap up 1" (25 mm) and press.

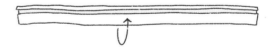

3. Fold the top long edge down to overlap with the bottom raw edge to cover it. Press. The folded-over edge should be in the center of the strap. The strap should be approximately 1 1/4" (3 cm) wide.

4. Edgestitch near the center fold, on the side with the seam allowances, so you sew through all four layers of fabric.

5. Repeat steps 1–4 for the second strap.

sew bag body

6. Fold the bag body in half with right sides together, press well, and pin in place if desired. Sew the bag body side seams with a 1/2" (13 mm) seam allowance. If you're making the regular (not 3D) book bag, backstitch extra-well at the ends that will be the bottom of the bag, to reinforce them.

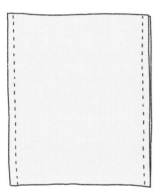

7. Press the seams open (to help make them crisp), then press them to one side, and finish the raw edges of the seam allowances together.

make it 3D, the simple way

8. IF YOU ARE MAKING THE 3D BOOK BAG, now it's time to shape the bottom of the bag. Otherwise, skip ahead to step 10.

   a. Pinch out a triangle on each bottom corner of the bag body by shifting the fabric so the side seams run up the center of the triangles. Measure across the bottoms of the triangles to find your seamline: make a 2" (5 cm) triangle for the little book bag or a 3" (7.5 cm) triangle for the regular book bag.

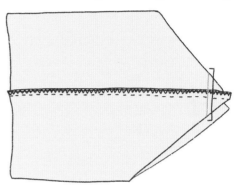

   b. Mark your triangle seamline with a ruler and chalk, then sew along that line on each side. Backstitch well at both ends of the triangle. Repeat for the second triangle.

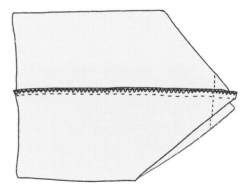

c. Trim the triangles, leaving 1/2" (13 mm) of fabric as a seam allowance.

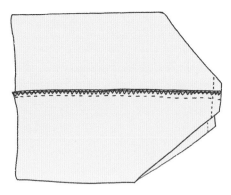

d. Finish the seam allowances and press well.

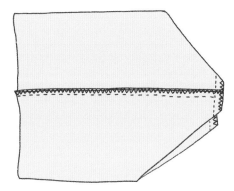

9. When opened back up, the 3D book bag will look kind of like this.

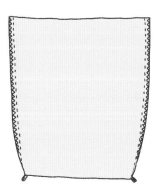

baste straps

If you want, you can skip basting and just slip your straps under the pressed hem, centered and 5" (13 cm) apart at the inside edges of the straps.

10. *For both versions of the book bag*: Turn your bag so the right side of the fabric is facing out. Make sure the strap guide marks from the pattern are transferred to your bag. Chalk will be great for this, or a little 1/8" (3 mm) snip in the seam allowance. There should be 5" (13 cm) of space between the innermost edges of the two straps, and the raw edges of the straps should be aligned with the raw edge of the fabric of the bag top. Pin your straps according to the marks, with the straps' center seams facing out.

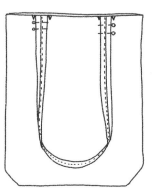

11. Baste the straps in place, keeping your basting stitches within the top 1/2" (13 mm), so they end up hidden in the seam allowance later on.

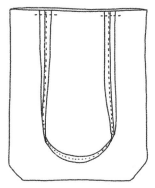

sew hem and straps

12. Flip the bag so it's inside out. Get the top hem ready by pressing a 1/2" (13 mm) fold toward the wrong side. Then, make a second 1" (2.5 cm) fold, flipping the strap over and down, so the raw edges are tucked inside the hem. Press and pin in place.

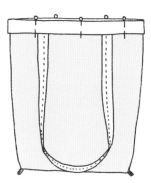

13. Edgestitch along the top hem all the way around, keeping your straps facing downward. Use a longer stitch length than usual (about 3 mm) for this.

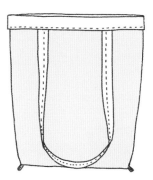

14. Now let's attach the straps securely. Flip them up and pin in place. Turn the bag right side out. From the right side of the bag, sew a very tiny zigzag stitch across each strap, close to the top of the hem. (Try a 0.7 mm stitch length at 2.5 mm wide or so.)

15. Press everything one last time. You did it! A book bag!

Chapter 17

Half Moon Zip Set, Flat Pouch, and Stand Up Pouches

half moon

stand up

flat pouch

Welcome to zipper town! It might sound like sewing zippers is hard, but you can definitely do it. We'll show you how to make a basic zipper pouch, and the rest will be history. Zippers everywhere! First, try the half moon zip, a tried-and-true simple zip pouch in our favorite shape, or try a flat pouch that's a total classic. Then make a stand up pouch that easily packs a lot of stuff and stacks flat when you don't need it.

We recommend cotton canvas, duck cloth, or similar, 10–12 oz/yd² weight (339–407 gsm) for best results. You can also use a thick raw silk, heavyweight linen, thick denim, or other heavy fabrics. With mid-weight fabrics, you may want to use a double layer: Simply baste your two layers of fabric together with wrong sides together and a 1/8" (3 mm) seam allowance around the perimeter.

These are such simple bags that fabric and zipper quality matter a lot. (See thoughts on bag fabric sourcing in Chapter 14.) For all of the steps besides finishing the raw edges, you also may wish to use heavy-duty thread, which helps make a sturdy bag that will last for years (and makes the topstitching look really nice).

no-fear zippers

Sewing a zipper is easier than it looks, but it's definitely intimidating the first few times. If your seam is wonky, you can always seam-rip; if your needle runs into the zipper teeth and breaks, you can replace it. It's super normal to be nervous. Using a zipper foot can really help—your sewing machine probably came with one. This helps you get your needle right up against the zipper so that you can sew your zipper with the correct seam allowance. Depending on the width of your normal presser foot, you may be able to do it without a zipper foot. Feel it out.

Always align and pin your zipper to the fabric with it fully zipped up—then decide whether you'd like to sew it open or closed. One way will probably emerge as seeming easier. It's important to do the aligning with it closed though. You can run into major problems if your project is fine-tuned and your zipper teeth end up misaligned. Then it won't zip at all! Use pins liberally—they're a great friend to zippers.

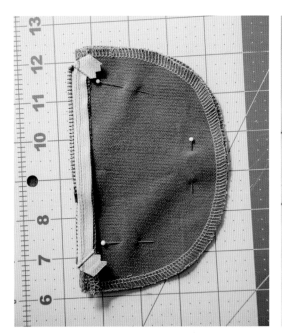

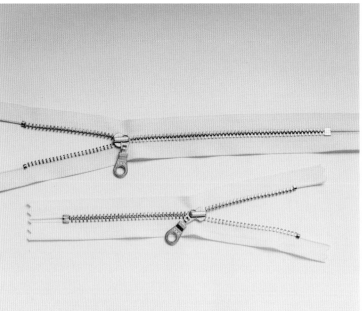

In most cases, you will topstitch the zipper on both sides after you've sewn it—this creates a polished look and helps keep the zipper tape and seam allowance out of the way of the teeth. Without this step the zipper may work well at first, but a fraying raw edge of the fabric beneath could soon cause troubles. We use one common zipper installation method for all the instructions in this book, but there are also lots of other ways to add zippers that you might learn in the future.

Finally, make sure to *open* the zipper before the step where you flip your bag right side out and finish sewing—otherwise you could end up "locked out" of your bag. Some zippers are surprisingly difficult to unzip from the underside. Don't say we didn't warn you! Ha!

zippers, and finding what you need

There are lots of places to source zippers. But finding good ones can sometimes be tricky, so here are some ideas for where to get yours:

- Shop locally. Go to your favorite small fabric shop or big-box sewing store; that way you can feel the zippers and find exactly what you want. Look out, though—it's hard for stores to carry a wide inventory of zippers, so you may not be able to find the particular size, color, or type of zipper you need.
- Wawak and GoldStar Tool are great sewing tool resources and both have a wide variety of quality zippers, and Zipperstop.com has a good selection.
- We've had a good experience with a few shops on Etsy—a surprisingly good place to look when on the hunt for specialty supplies. One shop, Zipit Zippers, has a really great selection and quick shipping.
- Lots of creative-reuse stores have zippers too, often for less than a dollar.
- Zippers can sometimes be salvaged from damaged or worn bags and garments too. Grab your seam ripper!

There are lots of kinds of zippers out there. Learning more about them can help you find your way to the one that will work well for your project. Here are some tips:

- With zippers, going with a brand name can often pay off. Generic zippers frequently lack quality. We've had great experiences with YKK zippers; they're the best in the biz.
- The length of a zipper that is noted in patterns and on zipper packaging or internet listings is the length of the zipper teeth, not the zipper tape. The tape will extend approximately 3/4" (2 cm) on either side of the stops at the end.
- Zipper teeth come in different sizes. The size is indicated with a # symbol. For medium to heavyweight fabrics, #5 and up is best. You want a zipper that will be large and strong enough to hold up to the fabric it's sewn to.
- It's totally possible to make a zipper shorter, though easier with plastic zippers than metal ones. Look online or in sewing books for tutorials.
- We recommend metal zippers because they hold up to years and years of use and look beautiful, but plastic zippers are great too and come in tons of colors.
- Don't worry about matching the color of your zipper tape exactly to your fabric. You may have to hunt forever for the right color, and sometimes stores only carry high-quality zippers in a few standard colors. The zipper can be a great place in your project for some tasteful contrast.

the half moon zip

The half moon zip is a simple project in a classically cool shape, a favorite pattern for a useful little pouch you will sew again and again and again. It is a simple canvas zipper pouch pattern in three sizes—tiny, tall, and big. Half moon zips make excellent gifts because they are super quick to make and really handy to use every day. Everyone on your list will love them! Customize with cool canvas, embroidery, block printing, patches, or pins—the sky's the limit!

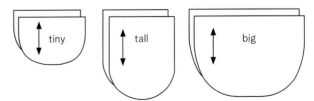

Half Moon Zip, Finished Sizes

	length (in)	height (in)	length (cm)	height (cm)
Tiny	5.5	4	14	10
Tall	5.5	7	14	18
Big	9.5	7	24	18

Half Moon Zip Fabric Requirements

	45" or 60" wide (yds)	115 or 150 cm wide (m)
Set of three bags	0.3	0.3

You only need a little bit of fabric for a full set, although we often make these one at a time, out of scraps. You will also need zippers: 5" (13 cm) for the tiny or tall zips, 8" (20 cm) for the big half moon zip.

1. For whichever half moon zip you are making, cut out 2 of your pattern piece from your fabric. Finish the raw edges of both of your pattern pieces using your favorite method: serger, zigzag stitch on a regular sewing machine, pinking shears, etc. *(Finishing will not be shown in the rest of the diagrams.)*

2. With the right side of the zipper facing the right side of the fabric, place the zipper along the top (straight) edge of one of the body pieces, so the zipper is centered. (One trick to find the centers is to fold the zipper in half and mark the center point with chalk. Do the same with the fabric.) Pin in place, folding the ends of the zipper tape up and in toward the center at a 30-degree angle.

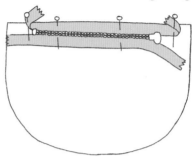

3. Sew the zipper on 1/4" (6 mm) from the edge, using a zipper foot. This stitching should catch the folded-over edges of the ends of the zipper tape and secure them.

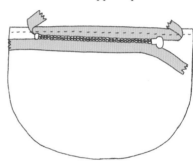

- -

TIP! When sewing a zipper, feel free to open and shut the zipper as needed to move the zipper pull out of the way. It's much easier to sew without the bulkiness of the zipper pull beside the needle, skewing the way the zipper tape lies. To move the zipper pull while sewing, plant your needle down, lift the presser foot, and open or close the zipper a little bit to push it back behind your presser foot (toward the part you've already sewn). Then lower your presser foot again and keep sewing. If the way you are sewing the zipper allows you to get the zipper pull totally out of the way before sewing, do that. Even easier.

- -

4. Repeat steps 2 and 3 for the other side of the pouch: Place the zipper (attached to the side that you just sewed) on top of the remaining side, with right sides of the pouch together. Pin the zipper, catching the ends of the zipper tape at the 30-degree angle fold to keep them out of the way.

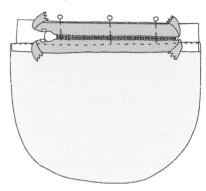

5. Sew the side of the zipper to the second pouch piece with right sides together, 1/4" (6 mm) from the edge.

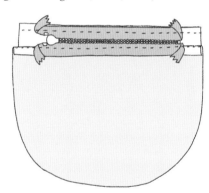

6. Finger-press the pouch pieces and seam allowances out away from the zipper, and press the newly sewn seams with your iron from the wrong side, then the right side. Take care if you have a metal zipper—it will get hot!

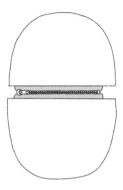

7. Increase your stitch length slightly from standard (for example, 3 mm or 3.5 mm is good) and topstitch 1/16" (1.5 mm) from the pressed edge for each side of the zipper. The longer stitch length gives a fancier look. Sew slowly and carefully, and be sure to catch the folded edges of the zipper tape at each end so they stay at that angle. If you mess up, it's normal. Just seam-rip and try again! Press once more.

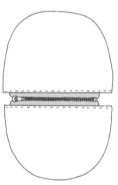

- -

TIP! If you're not using heavy-duty thread, you may wish to use topstitching thread for these very visible lines of stitching. Or create a similar look to topstitching thread with two threads threaded through the same needle. Wind a bit of thread onto a new bobbin and place onto a thread pin alongside your existing spool, then thread both strands through the needle to add a second thread.

- -

8. Switch back to your regular presser foot and standard stitch length. Unzip the zipper so it is three-quarters of the way or so open (so that you can flip the pouch easily later). Fold the pouch pieces with right sides together. Pin to align. We like to just use three pins to save time.

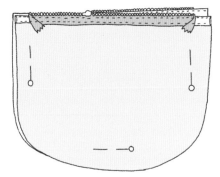

9. Sew around the curved edge with a 3/8" (1 cm) seam allowance.

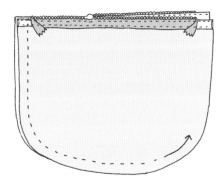

10. Turn the pouch so it is right side out and press the curved seam you just sewed. Voilà!

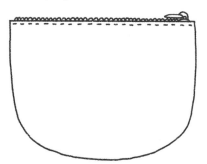

the flat pouch

The flat pouches are just like the half moon zips, but just have a different shape. Find the pattern pieces to make a set of three or draft your own by drawing a rectangle shape in the size you want, finding a right-size zipper, and adding extra room around the pattern edges for a seam allowance. These are a great way to practice pivoting at the corners and accurately sewing straight lines.

Flat Pouch, Finished Sizes

	length (in)	height (in)	length (cm)	height (cm)
Small	6.7	4.5	17	11
Medium	9.5	7	24	18
Big	13.5	9	34	23

Fabric for Flat Pouch

	45" or 60" wide (yds)	115 or 150 cm wide (m)
Set of three	0.6	0.5

You will also need zippers: 5" (13 cm) for the small, 8" (20 cm) for the medium, and 12" (30.5 cm) for the big flat pouch.

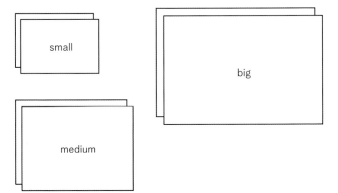

1. For whichever flat pouch you are making, cut out 2 of the pattern piece from your fabric. Prepare and sew, following the same instructions as for the half moon zip, steps 1 through 8, but when you sew down one side to the corner of the rectangle, lift your presser foot and pivot around the needle to make a crisp turn; then keep sewing across the bottom and up the other side.

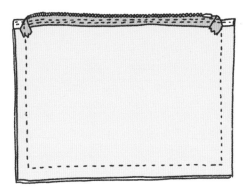

3. Turn the pouch inside out and give it a good press. A flat pouch! Fill it with some favorite things!

2. You might want to snip the bulk of the fabric off the corners at the bottom of the pouch before you turn it inside out, being careful to cut near but not too close to the line of stitching.

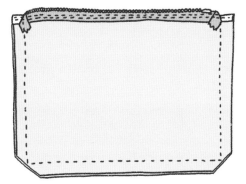

the stand up pouch

The stand up pouch is a riff on the flat pouch, but instead of two pieces, you cut one big rectangular piece (on the fold), and then you make a quick little fold of fabric on the bottom before you sew up the sides—the same way you made the fold with the drawstring bag (page 144), just more exaggerated. This creates a three-dimensional bottom that pops open when you fill the bag, letting it live up to its name.

Stand Up Pouch, Finished Sizes

	length (in)	height (in)	depth (in)	length (cm)	height (cm)	depth (cm)
Small	8.5	5.5	1.5	22	14	4
Big	12.5	8.5	2.5	32	21	6.5

Fabric for Stand Up Pouch

	45" or 60" wide (yds)	115 or 150 cm wide (m)
Both bags	0.8	0.7

You will need zippers: 8" (20 cm) for the small and 12" (30.5 cm) for the big stand up pouch.

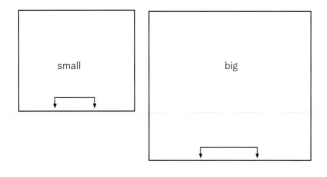

1. Cut a rectangle from your fabric for whichever pattern size you choose. Finish the raw edges around all four sides of the rectangle. (Finishing isn't pictured.)
2. Sew the zipper to the rectangle on one short side with the right side of the zipper facing the right side of the fabric; then press the zipper up so the right side is facing out, and topstitch.

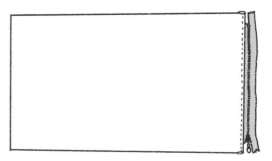

3. Sew your zipper to the other short side of the rectangle with the right sides together; then unzip the zipper to topstitch the zipper on that side. Because this pattern uses one big piece of fabric that is connected at the bottom, you will need to do some extra maneuvering to make this topstitching happen. It's a little like sewing through a tube. Just press well and sew slowly—you can do it. It might look a little weird, as shown in the diagram.

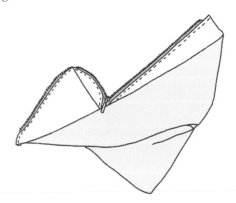

4. Un-tube and lay the pouch flat with right sides together. Fold the bottom edge up toward you 1 1/2" (4 cm) for the small stand up pouch, and 2 1/2" (6.5 cm) for the big stand up pouch. Pin the bottom fold and sides in place.

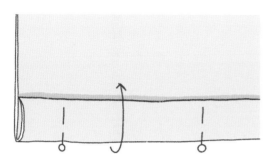

5. Before you sew the sides, make sure your zipper is unzipped so you don't get locked out of your bag. Sew the side seams using a 3/8" (1 cm) seam allowance, catching that bottom fold with your seams.

6. Flip the pouch right side out and stand it up. Voilà! A stand up pouch!

Chapter 18

Party Purse

The party purse is a boxy zip bag with a shoulder strap and interior pocket. It measures 5 1/2" by 7 1/2" by 2" wide (14 cm by 19 cm by 5 cm), which is not too big but still surprisingly roomy. You can leave the strap off to use it for anything else—like toiletries or pencils or keeping small things together within a larger tote. We like it in a thick dark canvas. Something sturdy! It also is quite nice made out of an old quilt, a bit softer but still fun and structural.

Party Purse Fabric Requirements

45" or 60" wide (yds)	115 or 150 cm wide (m)
0.4	0.4

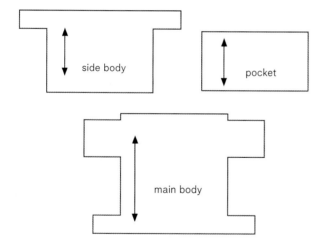

Trace the three pattern pieces (pocket, main body, and side body) from the pattern sheets, plus draw your own rectangle pattern for the strap: 2" by 46" (5 cm by 117 cm) or longer (see step 1).

You will need a 12" (30.5 cm) zipper, and some sturdy bag fabric.

make your strap

1. Measure and cut a long rectangle of fabric that is 2" (5 cm) wide by the length you want. Amy, who is 5'3" (160 cm) tall uses a 46" (117 cm) long strap piece that ends up being 44 1/2" (113 cm) long once it's sewn in. A short strap is good for slinging over a single shoulder and hitting at hip length; a longer strap is great for carrying the purse cross body. Up to you! We recommend mocking up the strap (in the length you think you'd like) with a soft measuring tape, and then adding 1 1/2" (4 cm) for seam allowances. Feel free to make it a little longer just to be safe—you will have an opportunity to adjust the fit and trim the length before you fully sew it in.

- -

TIP! If you don't have a long enough strip of fabric, you can sew 2" (5 cm) wide strips together and press the seam allowances open where you joined them.

- -

2. Follow the instructions for making ties and straps in Chapter 19 (page 183) to fold and sew the fabric into a strap. Add a second line of edgestitching if you'd like.

prepare pocket and other pattern pieces

3. Prepare the inside pocket by folding and pressing one long edge of the rectangle over toward the wrong side 3/8" (1 cm) twice, then edgestitch to make a double-fold hem; this will become the top of the pocket.

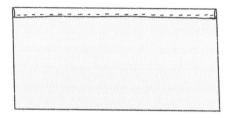

4. Finish the raw edge on the main body and side body pieces that the zipper will be sewn to. (*Finishing will not be shown in the following diagrams.*)

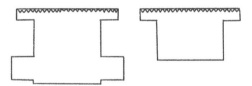

sew zipper

5. Sew one side of the zipper to the side body (the T-shaped piece), with right sides of the zipper and the fabric together, using a 1/4" (6 mm) seam allowance. Fold back the ends of the zipper tape to make a 30-degree angle before you sew over them, to tuck them neatly out of the way.

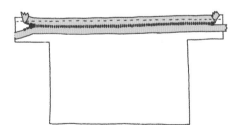

- -
TIP! For all these zipper steps, see more detail in the half moon zip bag instructions in Chapter 17.
- -

6. Sew the second side of the zipper to the main body, with right sides of the zipper and the fabric together, using a 1/4" (6 mm) seam allowance.

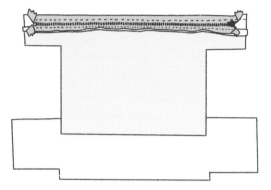

7. Press the zipper open and sew a line of topstitching along each side of the zipper.

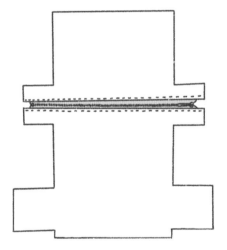

sew pocket

8. Fold the bag body in half, with right sides together, matching up the edges to create a flattened tube. Arrange it so that the main body piece (larger of the two body pieces) is on top.

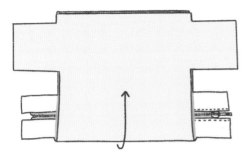

9. Place the pocket on top with the pocket's wrong side facing up. Pin together all three layers.

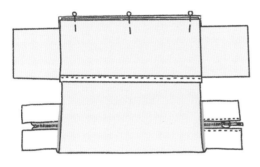

- -
TIP! If you're working with thick fabric and are not sure your machine will sew through all three layers, take a moment now to finish all the edges separately, before pinning, with zigzag stitch or some other method.
- -

10. Sew through all three layers (the two body pieces and one pocket piece), then finish the seam. (The seam will be hidden in the bottom of the pocket, so don't worry too much about how it looks.)

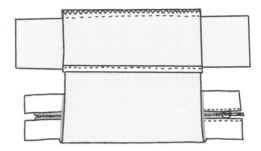

11. Now flip the pocket up and over, so the seam you just finished is tucked inside the pocket, out of sight. Sew each side of the pocket to the top layer of the body with a 1/4" (6 cm) seam allowance to hold them in place. You're working with a bag-tube shape, which can be a little awkward. Just pull things around to make it work.

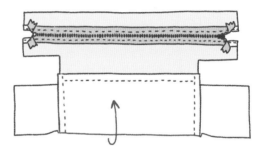

12. *Optional*: Topstitch along the bottom of the pocket, about 1/16" (2 mm) from the edge of the pocket bottom. You will be sewing through the body piece, the seam that's hidden inside the pocket, and the pocket itself—that's a lot of layers! You will likely have to unzip and flip the bag to get to the optimal way to sew this seam. This topstitching will be visible from the outside of the bag, so best to check your tension on a similar number of fabric layers before you do it, and lengthen your stitch length a little. This step isn't 100% necessary, but it will help keep everything tight and tidy and together.

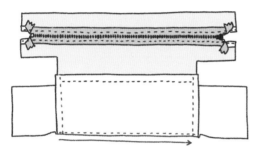

add in your strap

13. Pin the horizontal body seam on one side, where the ends of the zipper connect to the bottom of the body. As you align the seam, slide the strap between the two layers so that the strap peeks through the open portion of the zipper construction.

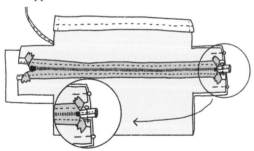

14. Sew this seam, and finish it. Twill tape or bias tape works really well for this and looks nice.

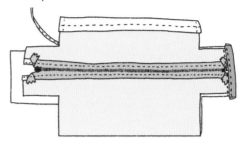

15. Now it's time to customize your strap length. Go to a mirror, put the bag over your shoulder (it's okay if it's still inside out), and find the sweet spot of length that works best for you. Think about whether you want to use the bag mostly cross body or over your shoulder. Once you've settled on a length, trim your strap and pin it between the layers of the second horizontal seam as you did for the first. Take care that the strap is not twisted. Let your strap come out of the opened zipper, to keep it out of the way. Sew the strap in place and finish the seam.

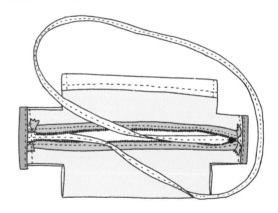

16. Sew the body vertical seams, all four of them, with right sides together and a 1/2" (13 mm) seam allowance. As you sew these seams, make sure your horizontal seams are pointing downward. Also, take care that your zipper is open so you don't get locked out of the bag! Finish seams as desired.

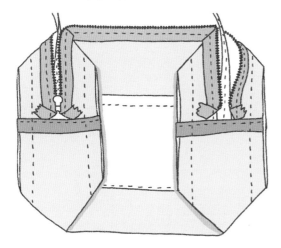

17. Flip your bag right side out and press all seams well. Use your bag for parties, non-parties, and almost-parties.

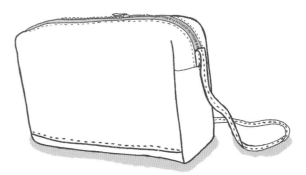

PART V

SOME BASIC SKILLS

To take you far

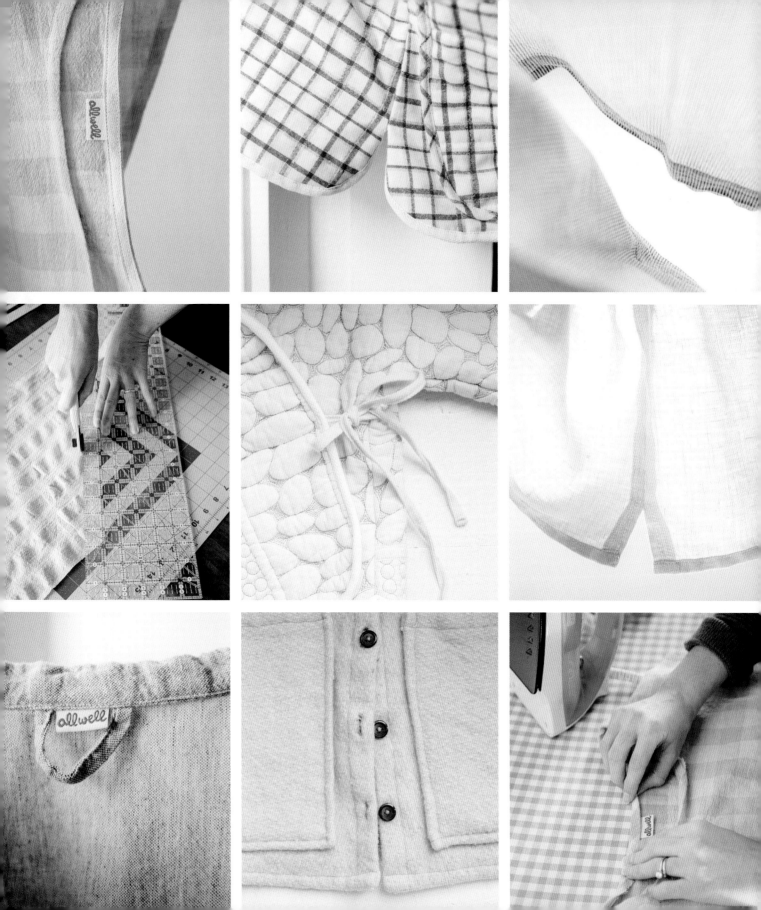

Chapter 19

Things to Use Over and Over

This chapter is full of sewing staples: techniques that we use so often that we wanted to really go into detail about them—like bias binding a neckline, or making bound hems, and seam-finishing techniques like French, flat-felled, and bound seams. These sewing techniques are beautiful and durable, making a garment that will last for years. There are also ideas for hems: split hems, high-low hems, making hems extra deep. Plus, ideas for pockets, closures, and tags. Lots of things that you can use over and over!

bias binding a neckline or armhole

Bias binding is, by far, our favorite way to finish a neckline or armhole—a simple, elegant finishing that brings in the texture of a bias strip, and gives a clean finish to the outside of the garment. We've used this method hundreds of times, and still get a little thrill each time. These instructions use binding the neckline of the box top as an example.

1. Gather your binding strip. If you want to make a binding strip out of fabric you already have, flip to page 176. You will need a 1" wide (2.5 cm) strip of fabric, cut on the bias (45-degree angle to grainline). The length of your strip depends on the length or circumference of the area you're hoping to bind. You can use a measuring tape to determine this, then give yourself a little extra on the ends.

   -

   TIP! With some mid-weight well-behaved fabrics (aka not too shifty or finicky), you can get away just fine with using a binding strip cut on the straight grain. This is a great way to cut out some fabric waste. It's one of our favorite secret tricks!

   -

2. *Optional*: If you're worried about your neckline stretching (like if your fabric is prone to stretch a lot on the bias), staystitch all the way around the neck opening of the bodice using a 1/8" (3 mm) seam allowance. A stretched-out neckline may cause it to stick up instead of lying flat across your shoulders and collarbones.

3. Keep your garment inside out as you begin to finish the neckline. This might be a slightly different method than you're used to. Read on.

   a. With right sides together, place the binding strip on the back of the neckline, near one of the shoulder seams. Do not pin the binding before sewing; it's easier just to guide it as you go with your fingers. Use a soft touch, being careful not to stretch the neck opening as you sew.

   b. Leave 3/4" (1.9 cm) of binding unsewn at the beginning of your seam. Sew the neckline binding strip (or bias tape) to the neckline with a 1/4" (6 mm) seam allowance.

   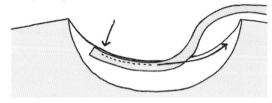

   c. As you sew over them, make sure the shoulder seam allowances of the bodice lie flat toward the back of the garment.

4. Sew all the way around the neckline. As you reach the end of sewing the binding to the neckline, flip up the unsewn 3/4" (2 cm) from the beginning of the binding, and sew the far end of the binding right up until your new stitches meet up with your first binding stitches. Backstitch to secure. The ends of the binding strip should not overlap at all; instead they should meet with right sides together and stick out perpendicular to and straight up from the neckline.

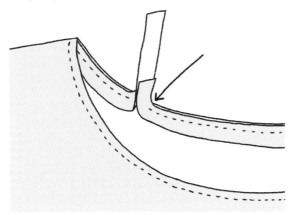

5. You will likely have a little extra binding on the end—trim the end to 3/4" (2 cm) to match the extra at the beginning of the binding strip.

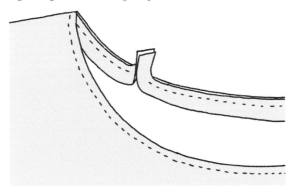

6. *To join the neckline binding into a continuous circle:*
   a. Flip the garment right side out, then fold the garment back at the point where the two ends of the bias strip meet so that the two ends lie flat on top of each other and stick out like little flags.

b. Sew the two ends of the binding strip to each other with right sides together, stitching a line parallel to the fabric of the main garment. Sew as close to the garment as possible without catching it.

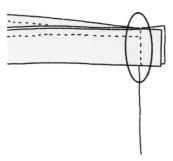

c. Trim the binding strip ends to a triangle.

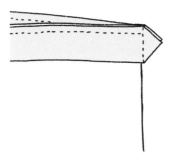

d. Unfold, flip the garment so the wrong side is out, and press the triangles open.

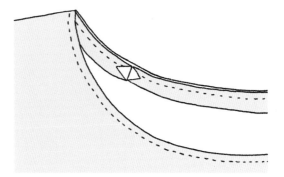

e. Sew along the edge of the neckline, over the pressed-open triangles, matching up with stitching around the neckline binding, just enough to tack the triangles down.

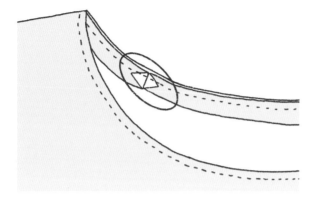

f. Double-check that your neckline binding now looks like the drawing.

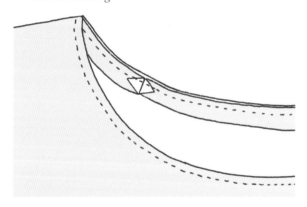

7. Yay! Now turn your garment right side out.
8. Press both the neckline binding strip and the 1/4" (6 mm) seam allowance from the body up, away from the garment, and toward the raw edge of the top of the neckline binding.

9. Stitch the 1/4" (6 mm) seam allowance to the neckline binding all the way around the binding circle, sewing close to the existing seam. This is called *understitching*. Use a normal stitch length for this—these stitches will be visible on the inside of the neckline.

- -

TIP! This line of understitching may seem superfluous, but it's actually super important. This neckline includes lots of layers of fabric all folded and working together, and the understitching is a foundational step, ensuring that everything stays in place through sewing, wearing, and washing for years and years. We've found that including this step produces a higher quality garment.

- -

10. Press the top raw edge of the neckline binding down toward the wrong side (inside of garment), to cover the 1/4" (6 mm) seam allowance and meet up with your line of understitching. This fold will be approximately 3/8" (1 cm) deep.

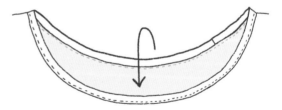

11. Fold and press the neckline binding one more time to make a double fold. The understitching will now be on the inside of the garment, helping you to make a consistent edge—it should all flip down quite nicely. Now your raw edges will be encased in the double fold of the binding and no stitches will be visible on the outside of the garment. Press the neckline fold well; use pins if needed.

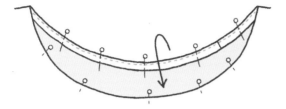

- -

TIP! You may want to increase your stitch length a little and check your bobbin tension on a triple-folded scrap piece of fabric before this step, since this edgestitching will be visible as topstitching on the outside of your garment.

- -

12. To finish your neckline, carefully edgestitch near the bottom edge of the fold all the way around the neckline. A beautiful bound edge.

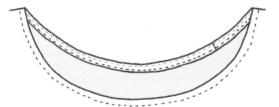

bound edges or seams on a quilt coat (or on a quilt)

The next steps lead you through practicing on scraps so you can learn to use double-fold bias binding, turn corners, and sew in circles. If this is your first time working with a lot of bias binding, you will probably have some moments of frustration. It can be tricky. Take breaks from your machine, breathe, take it slow.

1. Double-fold bias binding is a long strip of fabric, cut diagonally to the fabric grain, that has both raw edges folded in toward the middle, and is then folded in half to make a long strip of double-folded fabric. You can buy it or make it yourself (more on page 176). These instructions are for a 1 1/2" (3.8 cm) wide binding strip, where each fold is 3/8" (1 cm) wide.

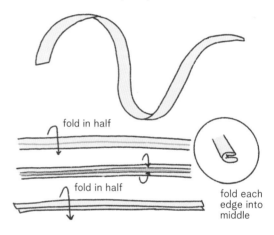

fold in half

fold in half

fold each edge into middle

2. Let's practice on a scrap of fabric cut into a small square. Begin by opening up your double-fold binding so it's unfolded and flat. Line up your binding so the right side of your binding faces the wrong side of your fabric at some point along the raw edge you wish to bind.

3. Leaving 1" (2.5 cm) of free unsewn binding at the beginning of your seam, sew your binding to the raw edge of your fabric with a 3/8" (1 cm) seam allowance, along the first fold.

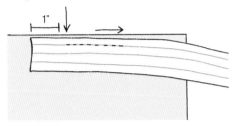

4. We'll tackle the corner next. Stop sewing when you're 1/4" (6 mm) away from the edge of the corner.

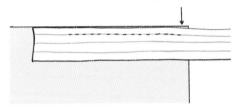

a. Keeping the needle in the fabric, pivot to sew diagonally to the tip of the corner. Backstitch and snip the threads.

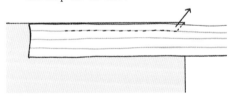

b. Fold your binding up at a 45-degree angle along the angled seam you just made; then fold it down to align with the second raw edge of the fabric square.

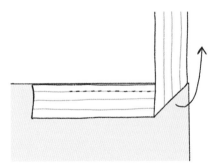

c. Starting at the top of the new raw edge's seam allowance, sew the binding to the new raw edge, using a 3/8" (1 cm) seam allowance. Continue sewing down the edge.

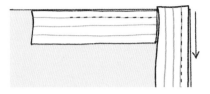

5. Once you've sewn the binding on with a first line of stitches, you have to take one more pass on the right side of the fabric to finish it. Fold the binding over so that it covers the raw edge and you can see it on the right side of your fabric. The corner can be tricky; fiddle with it until you figure out how it lies flat. Pin in place.

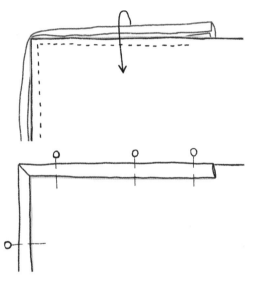

6. Edgestitch carefully all along the binding on the right side of your fabric, pivoting at the corners. Take care to align it well and sew slowly.

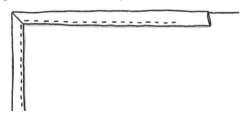

7. Now let's practice edgestitching circles, and how to end where you started. This is the technique you will use on the sleeve cuffs of the quilt coat (page 116), and also when you reach the point where your binding meets up with where you started on the main body pieces of a pattern. Cut another square or rectangle, and sew it into a wrist-or sleeve-sized tube. Turn the sleeve so the wrong side is out.

8. Leaving 1" (2.5 cm) of free unsewn double-fold bias binding at the beginning of your seam, sew your binding to the raw edge of your garment with a 3/8" (1 cm) seam allowance along the first fold of the binding. The right side of the binding should be facing the wrong side of the garment.

    a. When you notice you're coming up on the place where you started sewing, fold back that 1" (2.5 cm) of binding that you left unsewn at the beginning so it is out of the way and the raw edge of the fabric leading up to it is clear.

    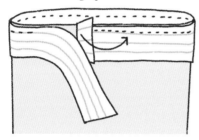

    b. Continue sewing all the way up until the end of the binding bumps up against the 1" (2.5 cm) beginning tail of the binding, and put the two ends up vertically from the tube with right sides of the binding together.

    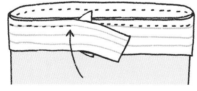

    c. Trim your new end of the binding down to 1" (2.5 cm) to match the first binding end.

    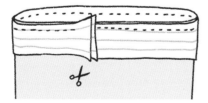

    d. Fold your tube (or garment) flat so that just the two 1" (2.5 cm) binding tails are sticking out to the right and the rest of the project is folded back to the left. Sew the two 1" (2.5 cm) tails together with a seam that runs parallel to the main fabric edge of your garment, as close to the main fabric as you can get it. Trim down the two tails into a triangle.

    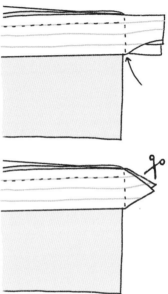

    e. Unfold the garment and press the two triangles open. Tack the triangles down with a few stitches.

    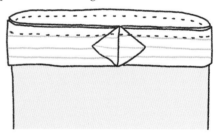

    f. Fold the binding over to the right side of the fabric, turning under the raw edge of the binding on the fold so the raw edges are fully encased, and edgestitch the binding to sew around the circle once more (the same thing you learned in steps 5 and 6).

make your own binding strips

Want your binding to match your garment exactly? Make your own binding strips! It's often cheaper than buying premade bias binding, if you're using fabric you already have. And a good use for scraps: Cut bias strips and you will have binding ready for a future project. The simplest way is to cut strips of fabric on a 45-degree angle to the straight grain of fabric with a rotary cutter, cutting mat, and ruler; or draw lines with a ruler and chalk and cut with scissors. You can sew strips together if you need more length—sew with right sides together at the strip ends and press the seam allowances open, offsetting the edges a little to maintain a clean edge along the strip once the seam allowance is pressed. You can also use a technique called continuous bias binding, where you sew fabric into a tube and cut one long strip. We have a tutorial on our website (*allwellworkshop.com/journal/continuous-bias-tape*) or search online. It feels a little like a magic trick!

french seams

French seams are an especially beautiful way to finish your seams. They require only a few extra steps and no fancy stitches. They make a very beautiful and clean finish because all raw edges are encased in an extra seam. This finish also produces very durable garments for years and years of wear, because there is less opportunity for the fabric to fray and each seam is double-strengthened. Basically, they're the best! French seams are most effective on light- or mid-weight fabrics.

Here's a general procedure for French seams—so you can make any seam French! You will end up with a final seam allowance of 1/2" (13 mm).

1. Align your fabric pieces with wrong sides together (not the usual right sides together). Yes, it will feel weird.
2. Sew the seam with a 1/8" (3 mm) seam allowance.

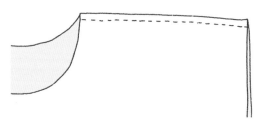

3. Flip your fabric pieces so they are right sides together. Press your seam fully inside out carefully so no fabric is lost in the crease of the seam. Because you are making two seams that work together, this is very important.
4. Sew along the seam with a 3/8" (1 cm) seam allowance, capturing the raw edges of the seam allowance inside.

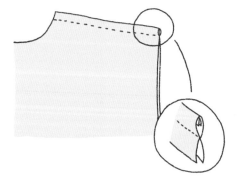

5. Turn the garment so it is right side out, and press the seams.

flat-felled seams

This is a beautiful and durable finish for a center seam, as a detail. You can also flat-fell the top shoulder seams and the side seams on the sleeveless box top or on ruffle panels, as well as on various spots on the cardigan coat (especially the center back seam), and on parts of bags.

Make sure your bobbin tension is fine-tuned when sewing through three layers of your fabric so the stitches on the right side look good. (When you edgestitch the felled seam, the edgestitching will become topstitching on the right side of the fabric.)

Increase your stitch length just a little for that edge-stitching step for attractive topstitches. You may want to test a flat-felled seam on a piece of scrap fabric before trying it on your garment. Here's how to sew the seam:

1. Take the two pieces to be seamed together. With right sides together, sew the seam with the usual 1/2" (13 mm) seam allowance.

    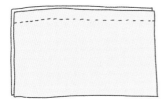

2. Trim one of the joined seam allowances down to 1/8" (3 mm).

3. Press the seam open.

    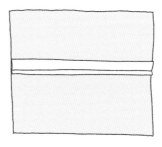

4. Fold the untrimmed seam allowance, the one that is still 1/2" (13 mm), *over and in half,* so that it encases the narrower, graded seam allowance. Press well. Your folded seam allowance should be 1/4" (6 mm) wide and should fully encase the 1/8" (3 mm) edge. There should be no raw edges showing.

    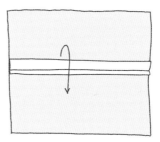

5. Edgestitch close to the edge of the 1/4" (6 mm) fold all along the length of the seam. This will create a line of topstitching on the right side of your garment.

    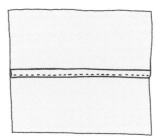

6. Hooray, you made a flat-felled seam!

split hem

This is such a good detail for the box top, cardigan coat, and any of the dress variations. (The cardigan coat is shown in these illustrations.) It's a fun option for styling, especially if you play up the depth of the split, but it's also just practical, giving more room for hips, or for legs to stride. Try combining this technique with an extra-deep hem and/or a high-low hem for more pizzazz.

1. Before sewing the side seam of your garment, finish the raw edges of the sides of the body pieces separately, using a serger, zigzag stitch, or pinking shears.
2. Align your front and back pieces with right sides together and pin along the sides.
3. Determine how far up the side seam you'd like your split hem to go. We like to use a 2"–3" (5 cm–7.5 cm) split, but the amount is up to you. For a 2" (5 cm) split, place a pin in the side of your body pieces 2.5" (6.5 cm) from the bottom to mark the place to stop sewing. For whatever length of split you'd like, add 1/2" (13 mm) to account for the hem. Sew the side seam with a 1/2" (13 mm) seam allowance as usual, starting at the armholes, and sewing down toward the hem. Stop sewing when you reach the pin, and backstitch.

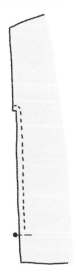

4. Press the seam open, including the seam allowance at the bottom that is unsewn. Press the unsewn seam allowance to 1/2" (13 mm).

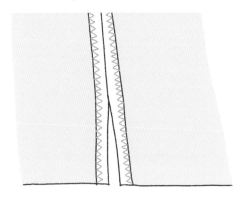

5. Starting at the bottom of the garment, edgestitch the seam allowance to the main fabric, 1/8" (3 mm) away from the seam allowance raw edge. Pivot to continue across the top of the split, stitching 1/8" (3 mm) above the split, and then pivot again to sew down the other seam allowance 1/8" (3 mm) away from its raw edge.

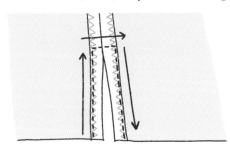

6. Repeat for the split hem on the other side.
7. Finish the hems normally, with a 1/4" (6 mm) double fold hem. Instead of a continuous circle, you will finish the front and back hems separately. Make sure to keep the corners tidy by folding in any stray threads from the bottom corner raw edges of the hem.
8. Yes! A split hem!

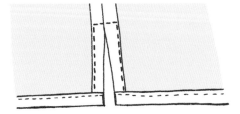

high-low hem

A variation on the split hem, the high-low hem can be used for box tops, box dresses, and beyond.

1. When cutting out your pattern pieces, lengthen the back piece as much as you'd like. Try adding 1"–3" (2.5–7.5 cm) depending on how dramatic a high-low look you're going for, or go for even more! Whatever feels right.
2. Continue with split-hem instructions (page 178), but end your side seam at the desired length, 2.5"–3.5" (6.5–9 cm) or whatever you'd like, based on the front pattern piece length—the back will be longer.
3. The rest of the process is the same as for making the split hem.

extra-deep hem

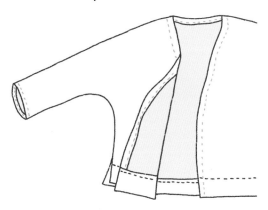

This is one of the simplest hacks, and one of the prettiest. Deep hems are a beautiful detail to add to any garment. They look especially nice paired with split hems (page 178), which will be even easier to work with a deep bottom hem. We like to use deep hems on any top or dress that does not have a ruffle.

add the deep hem

1. Decide how deep you'd like your hem: You may want to make your deep hem anywhere from 1"–3.5" (2.5–9 cm), depending on fabric thickness.
2. When cutting your fabric, use a ruler to add this amount of length to both the front and back body pieces, making sure to extend the outer lines along the same angle that the pattern piece is naturally taking. The bottom of the garment should always be perpendicular to the center front fold line.

sewing the deep hem

3. With your lengthened pattern pieces, sew your garment as usual until you get to the hemming step.
4. With the hem still raw, fold the bottom of your garment 1/2" (13 mm) toward the wrong side all the way around and press. If you have a very thick fabric, omit this first fold and instead serge, zigzag, or use pinking shears to finish the raw edge.
5. Fold again to the hem depth you chose. Press well, taking care to make sure that your depth is the same along the entire distance of the hem. (A sewing gauge is great for this, or a standard ruler works just fine too.) Pin in place.
6. Edgestitch close to the edge of the fold (or close to the edge of the finished edge for thick fabrics) all the way around the garment. Remove the pins and press very well to finish your deep hem.
7. You did it! Hooray!

patch pockets

Patch pockets are an easy way to add a pocket to just about anything. They're perfect for the sleeveless or long sleeve box top, the box dress, and could also be used on the body of the ruffle top! The cardigan coat has optional patch pockets, but you might want to choose different shapes, sizes, or add more, or make a custom patch pocket. Patch pockets are also *great* on bags. Add one to the book bag!

Suggested Patch Pocket Sizes

CUSTOM PATCH POCKET: Grab whatever you'd like to carry in the pocket and place it on a piece of paper. Using a ruler, make a rectangle or square around the object, giving it a generous amount of room, 1" (2.5 cm) or so, on all sides. Make sure your lines are straight and the corners are right angles. Then add seam allowances to the rectangle you drew. Add 1/2" (13 mm) to both sides and the bottom, and add 1" (25 mm) to the top. Cut out the paper rectangle with the seam allowance you drew. There! Your custom patch pocket template. Trace onto fabric like any other pattern piece and cut.

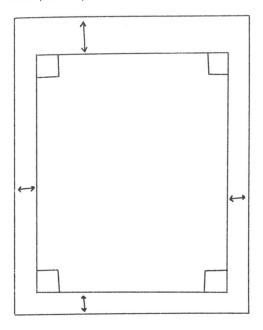

SMALL PATCH POCKET: To hold a granola bar, a small phone, a tiny notebook, some keys:
Pattern piece: 5" (13 cm) wide, 7" (18 cm) tall
Finished dimensions: 4" (10 cm) wide, 5.5" (14 cm) tall

LARGE PATCH POCKET: To hold a paperback, a large phone, a wallet, a bunch of wildflowers, your hands:
Pattern piece: 6" (15 cm) wide, 8" (20 cm) tall
Finished dimensions: 5" (13 cm) wide, 6.5" (16.5 cm) tall

1. Finish the bottom and both side seam allowances of the pocket as desired. We recommend serger or zigzag stitch, but you can also use pinking shears.

2. Press both sides of the pocket in 1/2" (13 mm) toward the wrong side, then press the bottom edge of the pocket up 1/2" (13 mm) toward the wrong side.

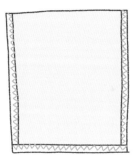

3. Press the top of the pocket down 1/4" (6 mm) toward the wrong side, then down 3/4" (2 cm) to make a double fold. Pin to hold in place.

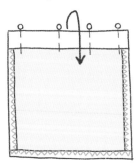

4. Edgestitch along the top fold of the pocket, close to the edge of the 3/4" (2 cm) fold.

5. Place the pocket on the garment where desired. The wrong side of the pocket should face the right side of the top. Pin in place along the sides and bottom.

6. Edgestitch along the sides and bottom of the pocket, close to the edge, starting down one side, pivoting to sew the bottom, then pivoting again to sew the other side. Backstitch at the beginning and end (at the top of the pocket) to reinforce the pocket. The pocket is shown here on a box top, but you can put it almost anywhere.

7. *Totally optional*: If you'd like, add another row of decorative stitches 1/4" (6 mm) farther in from your first edgestitches around the sides and bottom of the pocket. This reinforces the pocket and looks cool.

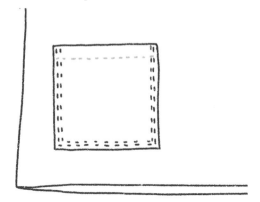

8. Voilà! Now repeat if you have any other pockets to add, or simply put on your garment and put stuff in the pockets.

belts

We love fabric belts—especially the look of belting the box dress. These instructions show how to make one kind of belt, but there are so many other simple belts you could make too.

1. Cut out your belt. The belt is 2 1/2" (6.5 cm) wide, but the finished belt will be about 1" (2.5 cm) wide. Belts between 50"–100" (1.27–2.54 m) long are good, depending on your waist circumference and desired style. To find your length, try tying a measuring tape around your waist, find a measurement you like, and round up to the nearest 10" (25 cm). That's a good place to start, but you can make your belt whatever length you'd like.

- -

TIP! Not enough fabric for a belt? You can piece multiple shorter lengths of fabric together to make the final length you need—this is a great way to use up scraps. Simply cut enough 2.5" (6.5 cm) wide lengths to achieve the length you'd like to use and sew them with right sides together using 1/4" (6 mm) seam allowances to make one long strip. Press seam allowances open—they will be encased inside your finished belt.

- -

2. Press each long edge of the belt fabric in toward the wrong side of the fabric 1/4" (6 mm). Then press each short edge of the belt fabric in toward the wrong side of the fabric 1/4" (6 mm).

3. Fold the long fabric strip in half, wrong sides together, so that your two long pressed edges meet up. Pin in place. Press the entire length of the belt.

4. Edgestitch along all four edges of the belt. Aim for about 1/8" (3 mm) away from the edges for effective topstitching.

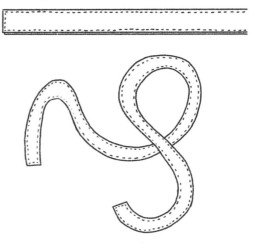

How to Play With the Look of Your Belt

- SAME COLOR OR CONTRAST? Do you want it to match your garment perfectly, or do you want to use a different fabric? For a bold look you could use a contrasting fabric. For a more subtle look you could use a tonal fabric. Or make a belt in the same fabric as the garment, which would blend right in.

- WIDTH OF BELT. Thin belts are cool. Thick belts are really cool too. The one shown is about 1" (2.5 cm) wide, but what if it were 3" (7.5 cm) wide? Playing with width is a great way to really change up the style of your box dress or other garment and experiment with volume.

- ENDS. The ends of the belt are another great place to play with different styles. You could go with the traditional boxy ends, or you could try curves or triangles.

ties and straps

Once you learn how to add ties to something, you can add them to anything. Ties are a great way to add a simple closure to the cardigan coat. You can also add them to simple bags to make a bag closure, or a strap for the party purse. Make your ties using the same method you would use to make double-fold bias binding, but use fabric cut on the straight grain. Here's how to do it:

1. For short ties, cut strips of fabric that are 13" by 1" (33 cm by 2.5 cm), however many you need. Cut a longer strip for a party purse strap (see tip), or sew shorter strips together until your strip is the length you need.

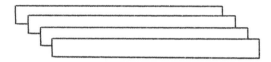

2. Fold and press the strips in half lengthwise. Unfold.

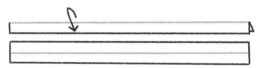

3. Fold each long edge in 1/4" (6 mm) so they meet at the center fold. Press well.

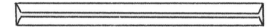

4. Refold the strip in half again to enclose the raw edges.

5. Edgestitch along the folded edges. Optionally, sew a second line of stitching along the other long edge (not shown in the diagram) for more of a "strap" look.

6. On each short side, press a double 1/4" (6 mm) hem to hide the raw edges, then edgestitch along the edge of the fold to tack down. (If you used bias binding to finish your garment, only sew one short end of the tie; if you're using this strap for a bag like the party purse, skip this step.)

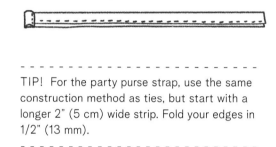

- -

TIP! For the party purse strap, use the same construction method as ties, but start with a longer 2" (5 cm) wide strip. Fold your edges in 1/2" (13 mm).

- -

hanging loop

Great for the cardigan coat! Hanging loops can also be nice on the box top, especially one you use for layering. How far apart the ends are and how long you make the hanging loop can be varied; it's up to you.

1. Prepare a 6" (15 cm) piece of twill tape or bias tape. If you're using bias tape, sew a quick line of edgestitching down the open side of the fold so the tape can't unfold anymore. Or use the ties and straps instructions (page 183) to make a shorter piece for the loop.

2. Sew your garment as usual until you reach the point when you're about to hem or bind the back neckline.

3. Fold the back of the garment in half to find the center of the back neckline. Mark with chalk or another marking tool on the wrong side.

4. Now, position each end about 3/4" (2 cm) away from that center mark, making the two ends of the hanging loop 1 1/2" (4 cm) apart. If you're bias binding the neckline of a box top, or hemming a cardigan coat, slide both ends of the hanging loop under the binding just before you're about to sew the last edgestitching of the back neckline tape. If you're using bias binding to encase the edges of a quilt coat or something similar, pin your binding onto the wrong side before sewing the binding on. Either way, position your hanging loop so it isn't twisted and curves nicely, then continue sewing the binding to secure the loop in place.

sewing a buttonhole

Buttons and buttonholes are a great closure for a cardigan coat or jacket. If your machine makes buttonholes, read the manual and/or look on the internet for some videos; then give it a try on scrap fabric. It feels like magic the first time you do it, and it opens up a lot of options for your ventures into buttons on pants or button plackets on shirts. We like to sew buttons on by hand with a needle and thread.

installing snaps

Snaps are a great way to add simple closures to a coat, cardigan, or bag and they work really well on heavy fabrics. For a garment, you can use the same placement and spacing logic as with buttons. Try on your cardigan coat to see where you'd like your top snap to be (likely somewhere near the spot where the front edge starts to curve up toward the neckline), and space your snaps about 3"–4" (7.5–10 cm) apart, moving downward from there—whatever looks good to you. You don't need a snap at the way bottom, just stop once your snap comes within 3"–4" (7.5–10 cm) of the hem.

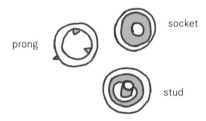

Many snaps will come with a setting tool that you use with a hammer to help you attach them to your fabric. For each set of snaps you will have two *prongs*, a *socket*, and a *stud*. The prongs pierce through your fabric and attach to the socket and the stud to hold them in place. Or you might try sew-on snaps, which are extra great for delicate fabrics. Use chalk or other marking tool to help mark your snap placement. Make sure to practice a snap or two on a piece of scrap fabric from your project to make sure you've got the hang of the setting process before you set them in your garment. Set-in snaps aren't easy to remove, so you will want to be confident in your placement and setting method before you start. But it feels so satisfying once you've got the hang of it.

the joy of tags

Tags aren't only extras, they're also very practical in that they tell you which side is the back of the garment. There are lots of nuances to how to insert a tag, and we won't go into all of them, but here are some general tips: You can choose tags that are flat, which you'd sew on either side with a short line of stitches, or folded over, which you could slip into the binding as you're finishing a neckline or add into a side seam so it sticks out on the right side. Generally, the folded-over tags are more common—they're easier to insert neatly without using facings. Take a look at some of your ready-to-wear clothes to get a feel for the kinds of tags that are commonly used, what they're made of (sometimes cotton, but usually woven polyester), how the information is printed or woven into them, and how and where they are inserted.

Tags are super fun on bags as a little visible design element and special finishing touch. Just slide a folded-over one between the two layers of the bag before sewing the body pieces together—use pins to mock it up and check from the other side to make sure you positioned it where you want it. Tags can also be stitched somewhere inside the bag, for a hidden flash of joy.

AMY: Oh, the pleasure of adding a tag to a newly sewn garment! For me, it feels like the icing on the cake—the sort of legitimizing detail that makes what I've made feel finished. There isn't anything magical about a tag, but somehow my handmade garments feel incomplete without one. It just feels so nice to mark what I've made as specifically *mine*.

It was pretty early on in my sewing practice that I got little "All Well" woven tags made. It's definitely an *extra* thing, an unnecessary expense, but to me it felt worth it for that extra zap of joy. It's up to you whether you'd like your own custom tags to add into your garments—and if you do, there are lots of ways to make or get them. You can make them yourself from a folded-over scrap of fabric with finished edges, or a bit of a selvage cut out and embroidered or labeled with a fabric marker. Or they could have no writing at all. You can also get premade blank tags that you can write on or iron a logo on—or whatever you want. Or, you can do what I did and find a company that makes custom tags. I get mine from the Dutch Label Shop, but there are many out there. Tags, like lots of things, are less expensive if you buy in bulk. Experiment and see if you like using tags (and if you like sewing in general) before making an order, and then buy at least a little bit in bulk when you do.

AMELIA: The very first thing I do when I bring anything home is seam-rip all the tags and labels off. To me, tags and labels often feel scratchy, visually obtrusive, or make me feel like I'm doing free brand advertising. With sewing, you don't need any labels or tags at all (if you don't want them). I love that. If you're sensitive about things like this too, a folded bit of soft twill tape or an "x" of embroidery is a good way to simply mark the back of any garment that doesn't have a clear front or back. *The joy of no tags*!

Chapter 20

Things That Will Serve You

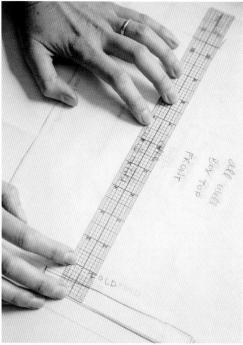

A sewing practice, like any other creative endeavor, is the sort of thing to develop slowly and very personally. You'll find the rhythms and patterns of working that feel best for you and the way your mind works, the way your life is. There are as many ways to sew as there are people—you will find yours! Here are some of the things that we've learned over the years of sewing as our lives and needs and goals have shifted and changed.

tracking your projects, and keeping a sewing notebook

At All Well, we are avid notebook-keepers/journal writers. This spills over into sewing—finding personal ways to keep track of sewing projects. Taking time to reflect and record also helps us learn, over time, what worked and what didn't. You might want to try it! You can use a notebook or journal to track, make a blog, make a spreadsheet, or use Instagram or another social media platform as a project log. Sometimes it's nice to collect your thoughts with a list of what you're planning to sew.

Make notes to summarize things after you finish a project: What did you change? What did you like? What did you learn? What will you do differently in the future? Did this give you ideas for future hacks and riffs off the same base?

Other things you might want to keep track of in a sewing notebook:

- patterns you have: what you've sewn, and what you want to sew
- common adjustments you make
- your measurements (updated frequently, bodies change!) and the amounts of ease you like
- materials on hand, and their cost and sourcing (fabric swatches)

A sewing notebook can also be a good place to dream and plot. Collect imagery of ready-to-wear coats and jackets and garments and bags you like for future inspiration. Make drawings and sketches based on what you see. Maybe you start to spot cool cardigans and coats around town, and that leads to ideas about how to hack the cardigan coat pattern. Even if you're not great at drawing, making sketches in your notebook can help you figure out how to combine elements into something you're imagining.

how to save a project

We all know that sinking feeling when you suddenly realize you've made a dire mistake or things aren't turning out the way you hoped. It feels so bad that maybe you feel like giving up—but hold on, there's hope! If you're mid-project and realize you're in need of saving, you're actually in a great position to turn things around. There's still time to do it, and it might be a small fix. Generally, taking a break will help, especially if it's dark out. If it's just a small mistake, maybe the seam ripper is what you need. You could seam-rip while calling someone to chat, or sitting outside in a park, or listening to music, or watching a favorite show or movie. If you've cut two right sides (a common mistake with pant legs) and are out of fabric, but it's fabric you love and bought new, maybe you can buy a bit more fabric.

Did you make something in the past that you haven't been wearing much because there's something not quite right about it? You might still be able to change it. Often for dresses that don't feel quite right, they need to be a different length—try using pins or clips and mocking it up in front of a mirror. If it's too small by just a little bit, you might be able to seam-rip the main seams, or just the seams in the too-tight area, and then resew with a smaller seam allowance. If it's too big, you might be able to recut the pieces and resew, or just take in a bit on the sides, or add a pleat or a belt, or do other small fitting adjustments after the fact. If it's just a complete disaster, you can cut the big pieces for scraps to use for something else and let it be a mistake to learn from. We all have those! Maybe that fabric can be part of a favorite quilt someday.

how to slowly work, and sew smarter

It's super easy to get intimidated because finishing a sewing project can seem so overwhelming. Try slowing things down, going step-by-step. Maybe you want to do a little bit each day, 10 or 15 minutes at a time. Maybe one day you print and tile or trace the pattern, the next day you adjust it, the day after that you cut your fabric. Then you sew the big pieces together, the next day you finish the neckline, then the arms, then on the last day you've hemmed it. That's one week's worth of days, just a few minutes of work at a time!

Our biggest tip for avoiding impatience: Have a really expansive definition of sewing. Sewing the construction seams themselves—like sewing up the sides and shoulders of a box top and seeing it take shape—is really rewarding, because you're putting things together and making visible progress. But it's worth it to do all the in-betweens. Find good fabric that you really love and are excited about. Choose your patterns, make muslins for them, make adjustments, clean-finish all the raw edges in some way, press as you sew. All those steps are *sewing*. We aim for the whole process, all of it, to be a pleasure, to feel like all that time was used well.

indie patterns

The sewing pattern industry used to be dominated by what is now referred to as "The Big Four"—McCall's, Butterick, Vogue, and Simplicity. These are the sewing patterns you can find in paper envelopes in the huge filing cabinet at the big box fabric store, or maybe there was a stack somewhere in your house growing up. There are thousands and thousands of them. There are good things about them and bad things about them. They're made by large companies that have been in the game for years. Indie patterns are different: They're made by very small design houses, often run by one or two people (us included, hello!). They're scrappy, personal, light on their feet. There's a wide range of what a sewing pattern can be, just like there's a wide range of what a book or a movie or a recipe can be.

Often each pattern will have its own hashtag on Instagram so that you can see the versions made by anyone who tagged it—this is an amazing way to gather inspiration and see specific feedback from others who may be sewing the pattern in a size similar to yours. And the instructions for indie patterns are often much, much more detailed than what is standard in the Big Four patterns, which can be helpful for beginners.

how to tile together
a PDF pattern

Indie patterns often come as PDFs that you download and print yourself. You can use your home printer to print the pattern on many regular pieces of copy paper, which you will then tape together to make the pattern. The trickiest thing with printing is making sure the pattern prints the right size: Usually you need to set a pattern at 100% scale, and just print the first page, and check the test measurement square that you can measure with a ruler. If it isn't matching up, you will need to double-check all your settings before printing the rest of the pages.

Assembly is kind of like a puzzle. Cut off the margin on two of the sides of every page (we like to cut the right and bottom margins), then align the alignment markings and tape the pages together into one big sheet. Watch a movie! Listen to a podcast! It's slightly tedious. Alternately, many digital patterns come in copy-shop size, formatted for large sheets of paper, which you can have printed at a local copy shop or via an online service. This will cost you a little bit of money but it will save you a lot of time.

tracing patterns
from existing garments

If you have a top in your closet that you really love, you can use it to make your own pattern to make a similar garment or use as a base for a new design. Existing clothing is a lexicon of inspiration! Like eating a delicious meal in a restaurant and then trying to figure out how to make the same thing at home. To do this, you trace the outline of your garment's pieces onto paper, add seam allowances, and then reverse engineer it to figure out how it was sewn together. Some parts of the garment will probably be tricky to capture. You might fold one pants leg into the other to get the crotch curve of pants. Or trace the corners of a patch pocket to get the shape. You can copy the outline of a detail like a pocket or collar using a copier or scanner, or you can use wax tracing paper and a tracing wheel. If it's something you have that's worn beyond repair, you can also seam-rip it apart to see the pieces individually and flat. Although we do not have space in this book to cover all this in detail, you can find more information in tutorials online or in books.

double-checking your
patterns with a ruler

A good habit to get into, once you have more experience, is double-checking your patterns by measuring them before you cut the fabric. Take a ruler—the flexible clear-grade rulers with red markings work well—and "walk" it along the stitching lines of your pattern pieces. (Not the edges of the paper, but where you're going to sew.) Is your inseam or side seam the length you expect, and when you go to the back pattern piece, does the back seam match the front one? (Generally they should match, they're going to be sewn together.) Check any outseams: Do they match? For any joined seams that match up, check them on the seam/stitching lines. Also check that the circumferences are correct. For example, is the circumference around the bust what you expect? It is especially important when you make any alterations or pattern adjustments to double-check your work.

speeding things up
with a serger

You definitely don't need one when you start sewing, or ever, but at some point, you might decide to get a serger—maybe someone has one to give away, or you find a really good deal, or you've just been sewing a lot and are ready to try it. The benefit of serging is speed and added simplicity of construction. Because you're clean-finishing all the raw edges of fabric in a garment or bag, that step ends up taking quite a bit of time—the zigzag and faux overlock stitches on a regular machine are many times slower and a little less neat than a serger. And, of course, finishing methods like French seams, flat-felled seams, and bound seams take even more time. Sergers, as machines, can just go really fast! Finishing edges is what they're made for, and they do it super quick.

If you have a serger, the order of operations is also a bit more streamlined: You cut all your pattern pieces, you serge *everything* that you can, and then you sew. That simplifies it. You *can* serge the edges together after sewing a seam (as most home sewing instructions call for in finishing), and sometimes you will want to, especially if it's a garment where you've got the fit dialed in. But usually,

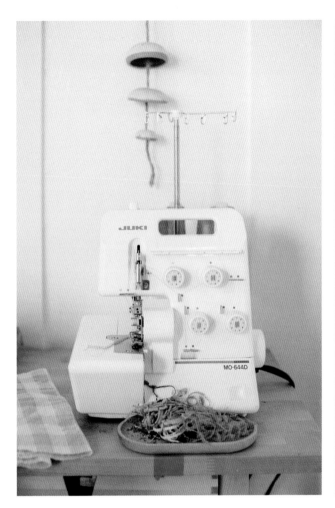

you serge first. If you're going to take out a seam, or a few years later you want to take in or let out a garment, you can redo just that area, taking out the construction stitches but leaving the seam allowances serged individually, and the edges are always going to be clean-finished. Serging first lets you do clean-finishing all at once and move on. Serge everything, all the edges, unless they'll be finished otherwise (like in a neckline).

pink serger thread

AMY: Over a year ago now, I switched my serger thread to pink to match a project I was working on. The next project I was working on wasn't pink, but out of sheer laziness I didn't want to switch back to white. So I used the pink thread, and I ended up loving the way it turned out. I decided I wasn't going to change my serger thread color anymore, I would keep it pink—and it's still pink to this day! Now it feels like a signature thing that makes my clothes *mine*, something unusual but special. You can find little flashes of delight for yourself like this one. There are certainly conventional ways of doing things—thread-matching being one of them. But you don't have to follow all the rules. You can use whatever color thread you like! Whatever pocket fabric you like! Whatever binding fabric you like! That's part of the joy of sewing your own clothes. There are no rules—only choices.

Chapter 21

How to Continue

prioritize by excitement

If you ever feel like you're adrift, here's a point to return to: Sew what feels really exciting first. Use the beautiful fabric, the pattern you've been looking forward to trying. Sew the item you really want to wear—even if it's not what was next on your list or what you feel like you *should* sew. Not every project will feel completely exciting. Once you're sewing consistently, it's likely you will have some projects in mind that aren't *as* exciting, but that you still want to do—that's normal. Get into the flow by starting with a project that draws you in. Then ride the wave to complete some of the less exciting (but still satisfying and enlivening) projects you have planned. And if you need a boost—just *follow the fun*!

Sewing is emotional! It's not *just* a craft, or a hobby. It might start out feeling like something you just do for fun, something lighthearted, but sooner or later, you will feel your *stuff* coming up. Comparison, perfectionism, feelings about your body, hopes and dreams that feel far or close, exhaustion, fear, ambition, loneliness, lack of resources or recognition, disillusionment. All of this is *normal*, and par for the course with any endeavor that matters to you, but it's hard! So hard, that you might feel like quitting. And that's okay—you don't *have* to sew. But remember too that no feeling is final. Once you learn to sew, it will always be there for you to pick up and put down—and the continuing can be complicated and nuanced. After the initial excitement wears off and the feelings come up, you will find your way through the deeper layers of building a practice in sewing, to the extent that you want to, that fits into your life and your hunger, your goals. Here are some of the things we've thought about and learned, some of the ways we've found new energy and excitement for sewing and have overcome the tough feelings as we've worked our way through, slowly, surely.

a note on beginner projects and what to do with them as you grow in your sewing skills

I bet if you asked any avid sewists (including us), they could tell you about an early sewing project that they're not so keen on anymore—maybe still sitting in the bottom of the drawer or the back of the closet, never worn or used.

Know this: Not every project will be a hit. Some simply won't be great. And that doesn't feel good, but it's also so, so normal—a universal experience. Just because an early project didn't turn out to be all you hoped it would be doesn't mean you need to throw it in the trash. Maybe the fit wasn't quite right and, knowing what you know now, you can make some tweaks. Maybe there's enough fabric to refashion it into a different kind of garment—from a dress to a skirt, from a long sleeve top to a tank top. Maybe you can cut the fabric into pieces for pouches or squares for a quilt. Maybe you can give it away to a friend who will really like it just as it is. Whatever you decide to do, try not to feel regretful or embarrassed. Making that thing helped you practice and learn, and that's *always* something good.

how to avoid making things you don't love

It's impossible when you're starting: You will almost certainly make some things you don't wear or use. If you're feeling really frustrated—sewing dark things in the dark, wanting to cry (or starting to cry), or finding yourself making multiple mistakes in a row, feeling angry or anxious—put the project down, go rest, go do something else. You can come back to it another time when you're feeling less out of sorts. If you've made something that feels strange or awkward, try it on with a few things you already have, and try wearing it a few times. Don't think of things as *finished* right after they come off the machine—be willing to edit a bit, seam-rip and sew again, hem to a better height, take off the sleeves, etc., until it really gets there.

permission to not love everything you've ever made

Here it is! Your official permission! YOU DO NOT HAVE TO LOVE EVERYTHING YOU'VE EVER MADE. There will be duds. You will be disappointed. There will also be big victories—things that turn out better than you expected. It's all part of the process, and we've found that understanding that and going into sewing with the mind-set that disappointment is a possible outcome really helps us keep our spirits up.

how to find sewing books you like, and an ode to the sewing sections of the library

We are huge fans of sewing books as learning tools, inspiration sources, and also just as general reading. The best thing you can do is take yourself to your local library or an independent bookstore that has a *great* craft book section and open a bunch of books. The library is often ideal here because it will have both old books and new books—lots of different ways of communicating and showing you how to sew. The 1960s and 1970s in particular have great diagram styles for technique instructions. You can grab an armful to take home or take pictures of the covers of ones you liked and keep a running list in your journal. Photocopy or take photos of pages if there's a technique or two in there that really helped you. And then, if you find a book that really speaks your language, you can buy it to keep on hand. All our favorite sewing books we found at the library first, then added to our home collections, knowing we'd use them a lot.

sewing friends

AMY: I first learned to sew as a kid, but I really grew to enjoy it while I was studying theater in college and spent hours in the costume shop, building shows. The sewing was fun (I made lots of wild things and learned a lot of sewing skills), but what was even more fun was being in a room full of people working on projects in parallel. Someone would bring a box of donuts on Saturday morning and we'd all crowd around the table with our coffee, looking at the plans for the day. Sometimes you'd work with a partner to figure out how to make something. The costume shop coordinator's name was Heidi—it seemed to us that she knew *everything* (and she kind of did, she was *very* seasoned). Someone would make a playlist for everyone to listen to, and we would sing along. A happy, bustling space, where work felt like pleasure, where any question could be answered and any problem could be solved. I miss that sometimes when I'm sewing on my own.

Later on, I worked a job sewing batches of custom bags for a marketing firm in Chicago. There were four

of us in our little sewing room, and between listening to podcasts or audiobooks in our respective earbuds, we would have long, strange, meandering conversations about anything. I started that job not really feeling like I had much in common with my coworkers and ended feeling a warmth and camaraderie that was encouraging to me.

I really and truly love using sewing as a way to spend time alone—I'm an introvert through and through, and I'm very comfortable keeping company with myself—but I also know from experience that sewing can be an incredible way to be in community with others. A common project or goal is always orienting and enlivening, helps friendships bloom. I'm grateful for those sewing spaces I have been a part of, and I want to always keep finding ways to be in rooms *full* of people sewing.

AMELIA: I also loved sewing as a kid. I had a little sewing kit and happily spent time creating "designs" and tiny doll clothes. My best friend C. and I made things like matching pencil cases in pink dot print fabric (basically the same thing as the Flat Pouch in this book: A staple). C. and I *still* love sewing together, mostly over video chat between Seattle and France. We hang out for hours: sometimes ambiently working on things in parallel and not talking much, sometimes chatting about life, asking each other advice, plotting our ideas. I do this with my mom too; it's really lovely.

Besides having fun, I've learned so much from sewing *with* friends: like with Sarah, drafting the collared shirt and pants and shorts and our other projects. Seeing how someone else does something! Meeting sewing people locally and through Instagram is always that special type of satisfying: Admiring each other's clothes and bags and quilts, getting to go deep on a topic that you've put a lot of thought into. Oh, how do you get your topstitching like that? Where do you get fabric? Do you want to trade? What are you working on? Sewing friends are the best!

taking classes

Want to sew with other people? Take a sewing class! Classes are an *amazing* way to learn, and a great way to meet other people who live near you and are interested in sewing. Look for a local sewing studio that offers classes or ask around at your local fabric store. A class can be an ideal way to tackle an intimidating technique or to try tools

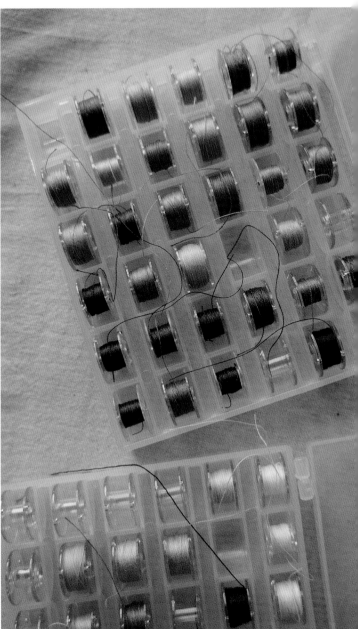

that you don't have access to at home. Seeing someone do something, then getting to do it yourself, and even getting feedback and help as you go: It can be so good!

There are also lots of classes online, as well as sew-alongs hosted by pattern companies or individual sewists that can have a class *feel* to them. Sew-alongs are usually free—so that's a perfect place to start if you don't have a big budget.

finding the ways you work and learn best

Video? Text? Library books? Blogs? Indie patterns? Instagram? Classes? Sewing friend hangouts? Alone late at night? One-on-one lessons? Sewing with a friend? Try a bunch of things to see what really feels best for you—where you feel most alive and excited. Everyone is different, and there is no one best way. Even the things in this book aren't the best or only way, as we keep saying. There are so many ways to learn, so many ways to do things. You will find what works well for you with time.

clothes are never perfect

You may be a perfectionist—not satisfied until the line of stitches is perfectly straight, until the hem is completely even. It might feel so important to match the thread color exactly. There's nothing wrong with striving for excellence—but take a breath and remember that perfection is impossible. Even the most couture clothes are made by human hands. It's beautiful that we can't make perfect things. If you look at store-bought clothes you will probably start to see errors or irregularities. If a garment you made has some imperfection, it probably stands out to you as glaringly obvious—but it's really likely that only *you* see the errors.

AMY: Once I realized that no one would *ever* look at my handmade garments as closely as I did, I started to be a lot less worried about sewing perfectly and instead found a level of "good enough" that I felt really good about. In some ways, that makes a garment feel even more personal to me, the places where I can see that my own hands made this thing. I like the little imperfections now, even welcome them. Maybe you will too.

refining your work

At some point you will have a handle on your machine, on sewing and cutting and choosing stitches and fabrics. Things that seemed confusing or daunting or annoying or pointless at first will start to come naturally. You might find yourself shifting to refining your work. That could look like slowing down and really choosing fabrics and projects extra-intentionally, reading a lot of sewing books or otherwise learning about fundamentals, taking time to learn a lot about fabrics and sourcing. Maybe you will want to tackle collared shirts and button plackets or pants fitting. Maybe you will get better at accurate pattern cutting and marking, or aligning the grain on fabric before you cut. Sewing clothes is one of those things that you can just keep getting better at forever. Follow your interests and let refining your work be a long and enjoyable process.

ebbs and flows

Some weeks, sewing might be all you want to think about. Some weeks, you won't feel the itch at all to turn on your sewing machine. Sometimes sewing will feel like the most exciting thing—sometimes other projects or just *life* will eclipse its importance. You can use sewing as an escape, or you can need an escape from sewing. All of this is good, all of this is normal. Be kind to yourself as your energy goes in and out like the tide.

little secrets

A special thing about sewing your own clothes is that you can add in little secrets that *only you* know about. Maybe a special tag sewn into the inside of a bag's pocket. Embroidered text on the inside of a sleeve cuff. A special scrap of fabric sewn inside a hem. A patch made from your old baby blanket. Sewing is intensely personal, and these sorts of things make it even more so—the sky is the limit to how *exactly* you make each piece your own. Sometimes just wearing things we've sewn feels like a little secret: walking around with a little glow of happiness. *I made this myself!*

PART VI

MORE

A few useful notes

Chapter 22

Everlasting Scraps

When you sew something, you almost always end up with scraps: bits of fabric that didn't go directly into what you made that are still big enough to be used for something else. Since so many hands and so much work and water and resources and care go into making beautiful fabric, better to use scraps with care than throw them away. This takes a little bit of creativity and energy, but it's a really special feeling to use scraps to make something new.

Our favorite books about food (like *Salt Fat Acid Heat*, *An Everlasting Meal*, and anything by M. F. K. Fisher) taught us to cook with a continuum of ingredients and meals and leftovers: A through line that pulls them along in time. The stems from some greens get sautéed with eggs and onions the next day, the leftover roasted vegetables are added to leftover soup with some more broth and a poached egg to make a variation that's not quite like either previous meal. A bottle of good vinegar gets used for many things. With sewing, you can find economy and a certain satisfaction in the thoroughness of carrying on that same sort of continuum, letting every piece cycle around and find its use.

The extra material from a shirt might be made into yards of bias tape that binds the neckline of other shirts or the insides of bags or a quilted coat. A deal on a roll of elastic might mean that you make several pair of elastic-waist pants. Canvas pants can spark a matching

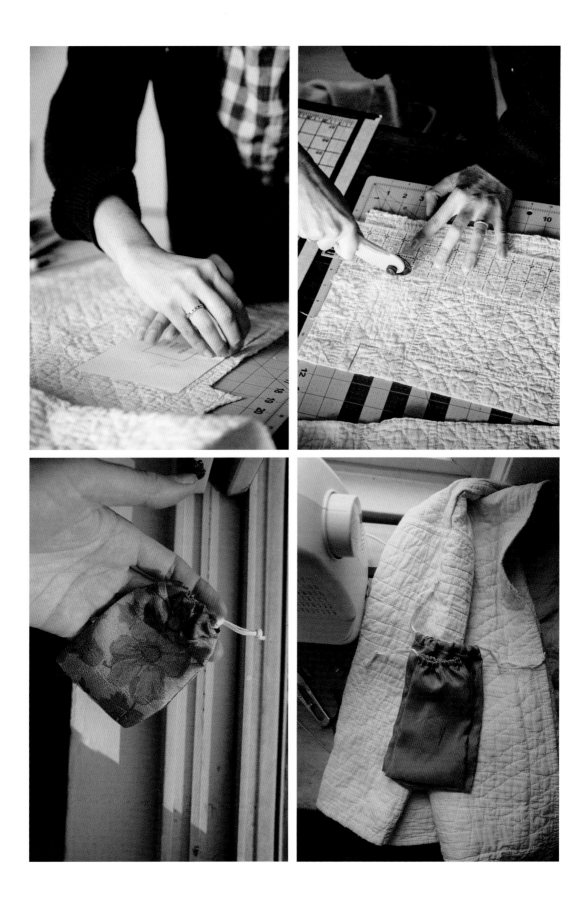

canvas bag of scraps, or maybe the inner pocket is a scrap from something else. Perhaps you make a quilt top out of all the small garment scraps after a long while, gathering them up over months or years. When we think about the possibilities of everlasting scraps, economy and thrift and secretly pleasing connectedness, sewing becomes even *more* lovely and exciting.

how to reuse and repurpose

Sewists can make use of things that otherwise might be unusable—like a damaged quilt or worn-out jeans. Get out your shears and seam ripper! Salvage zippers and hardware. Cut pattern pieces for garments or pillows or bags around damage or stains. Overdye the stained tablecloth and sew it into a dress. Grow your mending skills and patch some holes. There are so many ways to use things that already exist to make incredible new things. A quilt that was once too full of holes and stains to be much use as a blanket can become a quilt coat *and* a bag or two with some strategic cutting.

giving bags as gifts

A handmade bag is a really special gift, and an easy one to give because you don't have to worry too much about getting the size right—and a bag is almost always useful. Who can't use more pouches? Also, think about using a bag or pouch you've sewn as gift wrap. The gift is in a bag, and the bag is a gift too. Scrappy simple pouches or drawstring pouches can be great (and useful) wrappers or make a book bag to hold a book.

Scraps from garment sewing are perfect for making any of the little simple pouches, or half moon zips, flat pouches, or stand up pouches, or a sweet little interior custom patch pocket (page 180) for any bag. Drawstring bags can be almost any size—tiny ones are extra cute. Or, if you've been wanting a low-stakes quilting project, you could make a quilted bag out of scraps. All this is to say: Scraps and bags-as-gifts combine just right and are a really good place where you can practice your sewing skills and have something small and pretty useful to give away. Sometimes we even cut our scraps into bag pieces right after we cut out our garment pattern pieces, and sew our pouch right afterward.

sewing tools that you can sew yourself

There are a lot of sewing tools that you can make yourself, and most of them take just a little bit of fabric, making them perfect for bits leftover from other projects. Try searching on the internet for the name of the tool you want to make plus the words "sewing pattern" or "DIY" or "how to make a ____" to find instructions; there are lots of free tutorials. Here's some you can make:
1. Pincushion
2. Tailor's ham
3. Sleeve roll
4. Needle book
5. Ironing board cover
6. Pressing cloth
7. Square ironing mat
8. Pattern weights

sewing stuff that isn't clothes or bags

Clothes and bags are awesome, but it's also *really fun* and handy to sew home goods and other useful items. As you look around your home, you might spot things to sew, like pillow covers, napkins, tea towels and hot pads for the kitchen, or canvas bins or soft toys. These can be opportunities to do some fun figuring-out as you decide how to make what you're envisioning, to use a different type of fabric or materials than usual, to make a gift, to make something useful. And they are often really great opportunities to get the most out of scraps—either because they are small, or because you can make them out of pieces sewn together.

We also like sewing stuff that's not clothes or bags because often it's faster and simpler: A cushion cover without any closures is just a few seams; you can make it very quickly. And often there are fewer pattern pieces, no fitting or test garments to make, and you end up with something you use and are satisfied with in a new way.

Amelia often uses the U-shape scrap from the neckline of the box top to cut some stuffed animal pattern pieces, little bunny ears and bears and whales. Amy saves small scraps in a basket for needle-turn appliqué, turning them into works

of art. We both have kitchen napkins and coasters and pillowcases made from fabrics left from clothes.

a list of small project ideas, for scraps

Have we talked enough about how small projects are a great way to build your sewing skills? So fun, so low-stakes, inexpensive. (You're using up scraps!) Get that practice making straight stitches and keeping the seam allowance accurate, cutting and sewing and pressing. If you mess up, who cares? And there are literally *tons* of free patterns and tutorials out there for them, in library books and online. Many of these small projects are really good gifts. And, okay, yes, most of the bags in the book fall into the small-project category, but we wanted to give you a list of other ideas too:

1. Make bias binding, or thin strips of binding not cut on the bias.
2. Stuffed animals make really great baby gifts.
3. It's very fun to sew flat or cylinder-ish animals or dolls or fruit-shaped stuffed toys: Draw simple shapes and add a seam allowance. Or doll clothes. There are free patterns, paid patterns, or invent your own.
4. Kid projects in general: Draw and stuff shapes for a mobile, make a tooth fairy pillow, a pouch to collect treasures. Small-scale projects are very approachable.
5. Stuff to use at home: pillowcase, cushion cover, sleep mask, organizing bags.
6. Things to wear: scrunchie, headband, bandanna, scarf. You can match your clothes.
7. Kitchen things: napkins, tea towel, pot holders, coasters (for cups).
8. Patchwork out of scraps—maybe you will eventually piece together enough to sew a garment or bag or cushion, but it's also just a nice meditative project you can add to over time.
9. Sew all the stitches your sewing machine has settings for to see what they do. It's so fun! You will probably discover new things about how to use useful stitches and feet your machine has.

Also, just like you don't have to sew *everything,* you don't have to use all the scraps perfectly. You can find a place that takes fabric recycling, throw away small pieces beyond use, or pass them on to a new use by someone else. Maybe you want to do an informal giveaway on sewing Instagram, or bring it to your local creative reuse store, or hold a fabric swap locally. No perfect way to do things here, only a gentle invitation to look at what could be trash and see if there's another life hiding inside.

Chapter 23

Sustainable Fabric Sourcing

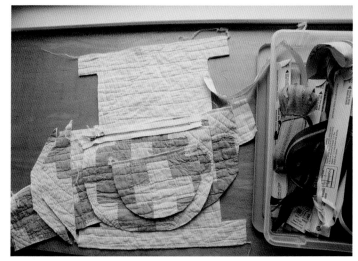

First, by far the most sustainable (and, often, affordable) fabric you can use is fabric that isn't brand new. Sourcing fabric sustainably might mean shopping secondhand, buying deadstock, or repurposing fabrics. It might mean sourcing locally, or shopping at small businesses. It might mean trying to only buy what you need, taking stock of what you have that you won't use, and sharing it with someone else. It could mean knowing and appreciating fabric and everything that goes into it, learning about how new fabrics are made and which ones are made with good working conditions, with the least chemicals and waste. You will probably find yourself paying attention, finding deeper appreciation—sewing as a way of bringing your attention and awareness to how fabric is made and how clothes are made and how you want to live. That's a good thing.

sourcing locally and secondhand

It's fun to keep an eye open at secondhand/thrift stores, and also at our local creative reuse stores. (Check if your community has one, they're awesome.) You might find groups online, like Buy Nothing or Freecycle, that can be places to find fabrics that other people aren't going to use. Or ask people you know: Maybe they have extra fabrics that they'd like to give away. (Have a fabric stash? Have any worn-out sheets? Want to trade?)

Other good places to keep an eye out for fabrics are garage sales, yard sales, and estate sales. Check local listings or just keep an eye out for signs. If you live in a city that has a "free pile" culture, keep an eye out there too. You might find some great fabrics, just give them a hot wash. Another thing to find out about: Is there an annual fabric sale nearby? Could you organize one for your area?

deadstock

A lot of the time, it's really hard to find fabric to sew with that compares to what you'd find in high-end clothing stores. Many amazing fabric manufacturers only contract with clothing labels and don't make their fabrics for the sewing market. We've often had the experience of liking a fabric in a ready-to-wear store, going to the fabric shop to try to find something similar, and coming up empty.

Keep an eye out for deadstock—which some fabric stores sell. Deadstock is fabric that is no longer being manufactured, often left over from a clothing label's garment production. Some fabric stores will have a deadstock section, and you can also find it online if you're willing to do some hunting. Or look for a fabric outlet—this type of store usually has stuff left over from the fashion industry. If you find a deadstock fabric you love, be aware that once it sells out it's likely gone forever, so buy what you need when you find it.

Sometimes, designers will sell their extra fabric themselves. You can also use eBay and Etsy to source amazing vintage or secondhand fabrics.

curtains, tablecloths, bedding, and other ideas for finding fabric

Beyond fabric stores, there are so many other sources of fabric for sewing garments or bags that you can find in unexpected forms:
- tablecloths
- bed linens
- curtains
- blankets and quilts
- towels

If you're in a thrift shop/op shop/secondhand store, take a peek in their linens and curtains sections; some even have fabric sections. Amelia has a thick cotton canvas curtain with a scorch mark earmarked to turn into pants, and a treasured box top was originally a beautiful cobalt blue linen tablecloth that had seen better days. IKEA is a surprisingly good source for fabric, if you have one nearby: linen curtains, bedsheets, and a section of actual by-the-yard fabric. They also have blankets (to use for a cardigan coat?) and other textiles that might be suitable to sew into clothes or bags. That goes for home goods sections of a lot of stores too: You can really find deals on new fabrics when these types of home goods go on sale, or when you find them secondhand.

You might not want to wear a test garment made out of an old discolored bedsheet, but it does the job for fitting and making pattern adjustments. And you can often find them cheap or free.

finding secondhand cardigan coat fabric

Reusing vintage quilts for jackets or other garments is an amazing way to give a new life to a textile that had been going unused. But this is another area in which to practice thoughtfulness and care. Quilts are blankets! If you come across a quilt secondhand that has no damage and would still bring value to you or someone else as a blanket, you might want to leave it that way. That said, maybe there's a quilt sitting in your linen closet going unused, and you feel that it would get more use as a jacket. By all means, sew away.

The idea here is to be mindful of what you're using and why, rather than buying up immaculate vintage quilts to cut into jackets you may not really wear. Always seeking balance! When you're shopping secondhand in person or online, keep an eye out for "cutter quilts," or quilts that are damaged or stained. These are perfect for cutting into clothes since you can usually cut around the damage. And often quilts are big enough that you can make several bags or other interesting things out of the leftover fabric.

on having a "stash"

You might start to build a stash of fabric without even realizing it. You pick up two yards here, three yards there, until you have a shelf or closet full of fabric waiting to be used. There are a couple ways to think about this. It can be really inspiring to have a shelf of beautiful fabrics at the ready when the urge to sew hits—we both have ones ourselves. It can help the creative process to be ready to sew at a moment's notice, without needing to wait and get your fabric before you can begin—even better if the fabric in your stash is prewashed and truly ready to sew. A stash of fabric is an amazing resource—but remember that the fabric is there to be used.

sourcing new fabrics

If you are hoping to shop sustainably when buying new fabrics, here are some strategies:

- Check out fabrics like organic hemp, organic linen, or GOTS (Global Organic Textile Standard)-certified cotton, or Tencel, which is derived from wood pulp. With the rise in recycled synthetics, there are a lot of low-energy-production options now available there too, although the long-term pollution effects of synthetics and microplastics are still a concern. And it's good to avoid rayon and acrylic if you can.
- Keep in mind that no mass-manufactured fabric is truly environmentally friendly—fabric manufacturing uses a TON of water and dyeing is dirty work, etc. This isn't to deter you, it's just to be realistic.
- Consume mindfully—resist the urge to build an endless "stash" of fabric, and instead buy what you need when you need it and use what you have until it's gone. Make clothes you really want to wear that fill holes in your wardrobe.
- Living in a climate emergency feels huge, urgent. And we've been steeped in advertising messaging around individual responsibility (e.g., "personal carbon footprint") that can lead to aiming for impossible perfection, minimizing everything to the point of inaction. Be gentle with yourself—you can buy the fun fabric! The weight of the world is not solely on your shoulders. Act thoughtfully, but be soft with yourself too. If it's easiest when you're starting out to go to the big chain fabric store to buy something that's on sale, that's 100% okay and good. Don't restrict yourself to the point of inaction. Remember, abundance! You're doing great!

Chapter 24

All Is Well

about Amelia and Amy

Amelia Greenhall (*ameliagreenhall.com*) is an artist and writer. She likes to be in the mountains, ride her bike, cook, and read lots of books. She has a studio called ANEMONE (*anemone.studio*) and lives in Seattle, Washington, with her husband, Adam.

Amy Bornman (*amybornman.com*) is a poet, designer, and artist. She is the author of *There Is a Future* (Paraclete Press Poetry, 2020). Amy began All Well in 2018 as a (very!) slow-fashion made-to-order clothing business, then shifted the focus of the project, in collaboration with Amelia, to teaching sewing and designing sewing patterns. She lives in Pittsburgh, Pennsylvania, with her husband, son, and big dog, Bobo.

about All Well

All Well is a creative sewing studio producing simple, intuitive, and super-hackable sewing patterns written with sewists of all skill levels, from never-sewn-before to super-advanced, in mind. We make the kinds of sewing patterns that can be sewn over and over without feeling redundant—often releasing Hacking Guides with our patterns to create room for lots of creativity as sewists approach the pattern. You can see this approach in action in our bestselling patterns and hacking guides for the All Well Box Top and the All Well Cardigan Coat, both included in this book.

All Well is also committed to helping sewists at all levels learn and stay curious about the craft, making sewing skills feel approachable, modern, playful and useful. Besides patterns, we're making creative and beautiful learning resources like zines, prints, tutorials, and other learning tools like videos and blog posts.

more from All Well, and where you can find us

Everything is on *allwellworkshop.com*—find our blog, tutorials, links to social media, videos, other patterns, and so on. If you want more process and hacking ideas (and a free bag pattern), we have a newsletter too.

some things that inspire us

- redwork quilts
- Alabama Chanin hand-stitched clothes
- poetry
- Gee's Bend quilts
- friends who are good at gardening
- Louise Bourgeois textile books
- swatches of fabric next to little sketches of what to sew, for planning
- small-press and self-published books and zines
- food documentaries
- Impractical Labor in Service of the Speculative Arts (ILSSA)
- looking at flowers
- "shop talk" of any kind/meditations on process
- a really good notebook
- fountain pens

be it ever so humble

AMELIA: In the scale of things, sewing clothes seems to hardly measure up as a response to life in a climate emergency, a mass extinction. Taking big-picture action feels important to me: marching, calling, writing, and voting. But it also feels good to do tangible things now: riding my bike, sending money to abortion access funds, making art, and publishing books and zines. Sewing is part of all that for me. A way to imagine a different future, tell a different story, to make something happen.

Sewing helps me counter the instinct to see scarcity, to see the world as a fixed and static thing. Instead: community, imagining, and building. Sewing clothes, like any other effort in the direction of abundance, makes a difference. Thinking about what world you want to live in, and taking action. A place to return to, over and over, be it ever so humble.

more warmth, for everyone

AMY: With sewing, and so many things in life, I want abundance. I want fecundity, flourishing, armfuls of new ideas. I want to leave feeling bolder and more amazed than when I started.

There are lots of ways that sewing can be discouraging, but I keep coming back to it with curiosity and hope. Life is patchwork in the way it offers itself to us. We always have to be piecing things back together. This is the case with big things—like partnership, friendship, work—but also with littler things like our hobbies, like sewing. And I think it's worth it. Sewing has given me a lot of purpose, a lot of rest, a lot of joy.

If you sew, you can absolutely set goals for yourself, hope to learn a lot, hope to make cool things that you're proud of. But we hope you will fall in love with the process. We hope you will feel good that you showed up to the sewing machine even when things don't turn out perfectly. We hope you will do it for the love of it. When you *really* love something, if you give yourself to it, it's abundant—it gives, and gives, and gives right back to you.